Walking Amsterdam
2nd Edition

Walking Amsterdam
2nd Edition

ROBIN GAULDIE

TWENTY-FIVE ORIGINAL WALKS
IN AND AROUND AMSTERDAM

PASSPORT BOOKS
NTC/Contemporary Publishing Group

This edition first published in 1999
by Passport Books, a division of
NTC/Contemporary Publishing Group, Inc.
4255 West Touhy Avenue
Lincolnwood (Chicago), Illinois 60646-1975
U.S.A.

ISBN 0-8442-2244-5

Library of Congress Catalog Card Number: 98-68299
Published in conjunction with New Holland Publishers (UK) Ltd

Edited, designed and typeset by Haldane Mason, London

Editor/Indexer: Paul Barnett
Page layout/Maps: ML Design

Reproduction by Dot Gradations, UK
Printed and bound in Singapore by Kyodo Printing Co (Singapore) Pte Ltd

Photographic Acknowledgements
J. Allan Cash: plates 2, 3, 4, 9, 10, 23, 26, 28, 29; Fleet PR: plate 21;
Robin Gauldie: plates 19, 20, 22; Robert Harding Picture Library/Michael Short: plate 18;
Roy Rainford: plate 32; Netherlands Board of Tourism: plates 1, 5, 6, 8, 11, 15, 16, 24, 25,
27, 30; Jeroen Snijders: plates 7, 12, 13, 14, 17, 31.

Front cover: The Westerkerk, Amsterdam (Travel Ink/Ronald Badkin)

CONTENTS

THE WALKS

ACKNOWLEDGEMENTS

Air UK and KLM Royal Dutch Airlines helped by providing transport to the Netherlands. Kirker Short Breaks arranged accommodation in Amsterdam and Hilton International provided accommodation in Rotterdam. Marielle Elbers of the Netherlands Board of Tourism in London put me in touch with local VVV tourist offices in the Netherlands; the tourist offices of Amsterdam, The Hague, Rotterdam, Utrecht, Haarlem, Delft, Gouda and Leiden provided a wealth of practical information. Many of their suggestions for walking routes have been incorporated into this book.

Special thanks go to my mother, Enid Gauldie, and father, W. Sinclair Gauldie, for insights into Dutch art and architecture, the history of the House of Orange, and cheese.

KEY TO MAPS

Each walk is accompanied by a map, on which the route and the main points of interest along it are clearly marked. None of the walks should take longer than half a day; most should take you about two to three hours, including sightseeing stops. All maps are drawn on a north–south axis unless otherwise indicated.

▪ ➤ ▪	Route of walk
▬	Major building
●	Monument or statue
▬	Canal or water
▬	Park or grass area

INTRODUCTION

Amsterdam is a city made for walkers. Within the old city-centre, traffic is light and pedestrians are respected as in few other European cities – though you have to watch out for trolley-buses and the ubiquitous cyclists, whose approach is rapid, silent, and unexpected! There are no hills to contend with, and most of the city's outstanding historic and cultural sights are packed into a compact few square kilometres. Friendly bars and cafés are dotted every few hundred metres, so there is always somewhere close at hand to restore flagging energies or escape a sudden change in the weather. Few Europeans speak English as fluently, universally and willingly as the Dutch, and communicating is never a problem. Nor is mapreading; the city's network of canals provides a ready-made orientation grid.

Public transport is efficient and plentiful: whenever your feet get tired there is a handy bus, tram, Metro train or canal cruiser to take you home. For trams and buses you can either buy tickets from the driver or conductor or purchase a 15-strip multiple-use ticket at one of the offices of the city public transport system, GVB. Public-transport maps are available at GVB information counters. Amsterdam's mass-transit system is divided into zones; all the walks described in this book start and end within the central zone.

You can save money by buying an Amsterdam Culture and Leisure Pass. This carnet of 28 coupons currently costs 29.90 guilders and gives free entry to many of Amsterdam's museums and attractions, including the Rijksmuseum, Van Gogh Museum, Stedelijk Museum of Modern Art, Amsterdam Historical Museum, Rembrandt's House and the Willet–Holthuysen, and a minimum 25 per cent discount on entry to the Dutch Maritime Museum, Tropical Museum, Madame Tussaud Scenerama and the Sloten Windmill. Other benefits include cut-price day tickets on the Museum Boat and Canal Bus ferries and special offers at restaurants and cafés around the city.

Equally walker-friendly are the historic Randstadt towns which ring Amsterdam. The best way to get to these is by rail. Trains are fast and frequent. None of the towns chosen is more than an hour from Amsterdam by train; most are less than 45 minutes away. All will repay a day's outing.

Dutch weather can change from warm and sunny to chilly and wet in the blink of an eye, even in high summer. Pack a light waterproof or carry an umbrella. Winters are cold; warm clothes, waterproof footwear, hats and gloves are recommended from October until the end of April. The best walking months are between mid-April and mid-October.

This book includes a varied menu of walks for all seasons, from longer rambles in parks and countryside to shorter city-centre itineraries with plenty of breaks in museums, art galleries and historic buildings. Some walks can be paired up to give a longer itinerary.

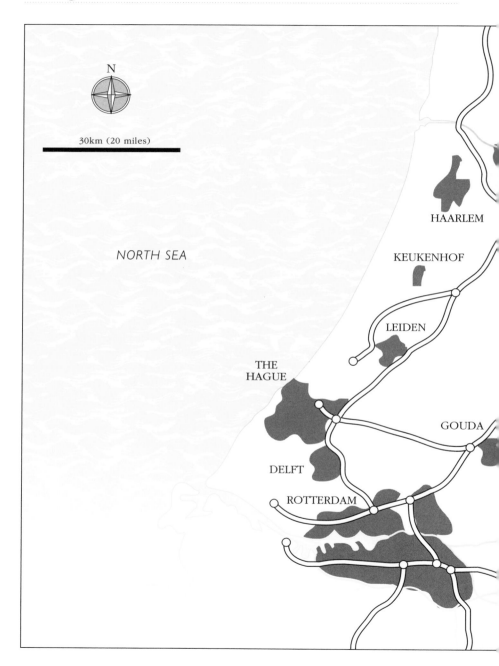

N

30km (20 miles)

NORTH SEA

HAARLEM

KEUKENHOF

LEIDEN

THE
HAGUE

GOUDA

DELFT

ROTTERDAM

MARKERMEER

AMSTERDAM

UTRECHT

LEK

WAAL

MAAS

A CITY'S HISTORY

Amsterdam is an upstart among the great cities of Europe. Most of the buildings you will see on your walks around the city date from no earlier than the 17th century. On the other hand, much of the city's historic heart survives intact or restored, with surprisingly little modern intrusion.

In prehistoric and Roman times, and through the Dark Ages, the site on which the city now stands was empty marshland between the North Sea and the waters of the Ij and the Amstel. Later it became a small fishing settlement. By the early 13th century it had grown into a prosperous little merchant town within the territory of the Bishops of Utrecht, who ceded it in 1313 to the Count of Holland.

THE CITY AND THE SEA

At the same time the city had to battle another antagonist: the North Sea. Though the sea brought prosperity, it continually threatened to overwhelm the city and the farmland around it. Stubbornness and ingenuity pushed the sea back: with the introduction of steam-driven pumping engines in the 19th century the tide finally turned in favour of the Amsterdammers.

This struggle with the sea shaped Amsterdam. Land for building was always in short supply, so houses are squeezed side by side along the canals. These buildings are narrow, five and six storeys high, and set on a foundation of piles driven through the soft surface to the hard ground below. Inevitably, some have subsided with the passage of time; today you can see many older buildings leaning drunkenly against their neighbours.

The sea gave Amsterdam a highway to ports all over Europe, while the rivers carried its trade goods far inland. Through the Middle Ages Amsterdam's prosperity was boosted by commerce, first with other North Sea ports, then with the Baltic and ever further afield. By the mid-15th century it had become the most important port in northern Europe, trading across the length and breadth of the mighty Holy Roman Empire. In 1489 the Emperor Maximilian I (1459–1519) granted it the imperial seal. With a population of 9000, it was one of the biggest cities in Europe.

Reformation and revolution
The radical ideas of the Protestant Reformation were quickly taken up by traditionally independent-minded and tolerant Amsterdammers. The city, now ruled by Philip II of Spain (1527–1598), patron of the notorious Spanish Inquisition, nevertheless became a refuge for Protestants from less liberal parts of the continent. Dissidence turned to armed resistance in 1568, following the brutal occupation of Amsterdam by the Spanish Duke of

Alva (1508–1582). Led by the Protestant Duke William of Orange (1533–1584) – William the Silent – the rebels evicted Alva's Spanish army from the surrounding provinces and besieged Amsterdam, which eventually surrendered to William in 1578.

The Golden Age

The overthrow of Spanish rule ushered in a Golden Age for Amsterdam and the Dutch Republic. Its greatest former rival, Antwerp, having backed the Spanish side, had been sacked following the siege of 1584–5; refugees from there brought wealth and new skills to Amsterdam. The city became a haven for painters and philosophers.

By the mid-17th century Amsterdam was home to more than 200,000 people. The city had already taken on its modern form. Work began as early as 1613 on the three canal rings – Herengracht, Keizersgracht and Prinsengracht – which today separate historic Amsterdam from the later outer suburbs. Rich merchants built luxurious townhouses along the new canals, and their wealth trickled down to painters and craftsmen. The élite commissioned Rembrandt and his peers, but ordinary folk could afford the cheaper work of hacks of the artists' guild. Visitors were awed by the city's prosperity, clean streets and public works; by 1670, when cities like London and Paris were mostly sewage-scented slums, Amsterdam boasted streets lit each night by 2000 oil lanterns.

The war with Philip II had closed the ports of Spain and Portugal to Dutch traders, who promptly set out to forge their own trade routes to the New World. In 1595 Cornelis de Houtman (*c*.1540–1599) launched an expedition break the Spanish–Portuguese monopoly of the hugely profitable trade routes to the East Indies. Two successful voyages triggered a stampede to get into the trade. In 1602 the rival merchants agreed to stop cutting each other's throats and formed instead the United East India Company (Vereinigde Oostindische Compagnie). With its own navy and army to protect its ships and factories, the VOC was enormously powerful and incredibly wealthy.

In the 17th and 18th centuries came wars with England and France sapped the country's energies and drained its coffers. In 1795 revolutionaries backed by the new French Republic overthrew the government of the Stadhouder William V (1748–1806) and the States-General and declared a Batavian Republic. This was soon swept away and Louis Bonaparte (1778–1846) was installed as King of the Netherlands.

The 19th century

With the Bonapartist star waning, William V's son William (1772–1843) returned in 1813 to become, in 1815, King William I of an expanded Netherlands, which from 1814 included for the first time the southern provinces (now Belgium). The union was not to last long; in 1831–2 the southern provinces rose in revolt and Belgium became an independent kingdom (Luxembourg followed suit in 1867). The age of steam made Amsterdam a vital link between Europe's booming railway networks and the transatlantic liner and freight services, while wealth poured into the city from the newly discovered South African diamond mines.

Occupation and liberation

Germany occupied the Netherlands during World War II. By 1941 the occupiers had begun rounding up Amsterdam's Jewish citizens for transportation to concentration camps in Germany and Poland. Underground resistance groups and individuals helped shelter Jews and other fugitives. Allied troops liberated the Netherlands in May 1945, arriving in Amsterdam on 7 May, only a few days before the German surrender and the end of the war in Europe.

AMSTERDAM TODAY

The modern city of Amsterdam is a mixture of bohemianism, sleaze and stolid respectability. On the Old Side, it is not unusual to see an elderly housewife carrying her shopping into an apartment doorway flanked on one side by a neon-lit window in which a plump prostitute displays her charms and on the other by a 'coffee shop' where the fumes of hash are heavy on the air. The age-old tradition of turning a blind eye continues to thrive.

The compact city-centre – within the ring of the inner Singel Canal – buzzes with tourism year-round, but the heart of the city is still very much a place where local people live, work and play. In the more modern suburbs outside the old city-centre – and even in the Jordaan and the harbour neighbourhoods – there is hardly a visitor in sight.

KEY DATES AND PEOPLE

- Around 1000: Earliest primitive settlements around the Amstel
- 11th century: Gijsbrecht van Aemstel builds castle on banks of the Amstel
- 1300: Gijsbrecht IV ousted by Bishop of Utrecht
- 1317: Amsterdam granted to William, Count of Holland
- Mid-15th century: Amsterdam established as major merchant city; Netherlands ruled by succession of Hapsburg princes and princesses
- 1517: Beginning of the Protestant Reformation in Germany; Lutheran and Calvinist ideas popularized in Amsterdam and the Netherlands
- 1565: Birth of Hendrick de Keyser (died 1621)
- 1566: Protestant iconoclasts smash statues and burn churches. Philip II of Spain, now ruler of the Low Countries, sends 10,000 troops under the Duke of Alva
- 1567: Reign of terror; Alva's 'Council of Blood' executes thousands of Protestants, and many more flee to England or France
- 1568: William the Silent defeated in attempt to drive out Spaniards; Eighty Years' War begins
- 1572: William begins campaign of naval guerrilla warfare; most Randstadt towns fall into rebel Dutch hands
- 1572–3: Rebel towns besieged, then relieved by William; Amsterdam remains in Spanish hands

- 1575–6: William besieges Amsterdam
- 1578: Amsterdam yields to William
- 1579–1609: Catholic southern provinces side with Spain (Union of Arras); northern provinces form Union of Utrecht, and decades of war follow
- 1581: Northern provinces renounce allegiance to Spain and declare republic ruled by the States General (made up of representatives of each of the seven provinces, called Advocates) and the Stadhouder, William the Silent
- 1584: William the Silent assassinated; Maurice of Nassau (1567–1625) becomes Stadhouder
- 1585: Birth in Haarlem of Frans Hals (died 1666)
- 1586–1618: Johan (Jan) van Oldenbarneveldt (1547–1619), Advocate of province of Holland, dominates civil wing of government
- 1602: Dutch East India Company formed
- 1606: Birth in Leiden of Rembrandt van Rijn (died 1669)
- 1609: Twelve Years' Truce signed with Spain, recognizing Dutch independence and ushering in Amsterdam's Golden Age of prosperity
- 1621: Renewed hostilities; Thirty Years' War involves much of Europe
- 1624: Dutch West India Company formed
- 1632: Birth in Delft of Jan Vermeer (died 1675)
- 1648: Peace of Westphalia ends Thirty Years' War
- 1651–53: War with England
- 1689: Deposition of James II & VII of

England and Scotland (1633–1701); Stadhouder Prince William III of Orange (1650–1702), through his wife Mary Stuart (1662–1694), invited to become King William III of England and Scotland
- 1701–14: Netherlands involved in War of Spanish Succession against France
- 1787: Patriot rising crushed in Amsterdam
- 1795: French Revolutionary Army occupies Amsterdam and Netherlands with widespread popular support
- 1806: Napoleon places younger brother Louis Bonaparte on the throne
- 1813: French withdrawal; return of Stadhouder William VI, who becomes King William I of the Netherlands
- 1848–49: Parliamentary reform, carried out by Johan Rudolf Thorbecke (1798–1872) to avert revolution, widens franchise
- 1853: Birth in Zundert of Vincent Van Gogh (died 1890)
- 1872: Birth in Amersfoort of Piet Mondrian (died 1944)
- 1914–18: Netherlands preserves neutrality in World War I
- 1940–45: German Occupation
- 1940s–50s: Netherlands withdraws from overseas empire; completion of Zuiderzee reclamation
- 1960s–70s: Liberal city regime in Amsterdam makes it a gathering place for artists and bohemians from all over Europe
- 1980s: Squatters oppose demolition of housing in city-centre to make way for office blocks

CATEGORIES OF WALKS

Museum Walks
- Prinsengracht: *Noorderkerk to Weesperplein*
- Rijksmuseum and the Vondelpark
- Westelijk Eilanden: *The Western Islands*
- The Hague 1: *Historic Buildings*
- Rotterdam 2: *Parks and museums*
- Haarlem 2: *Museums and monuments*
- Leiden 3: *Museums*

Canal and River Walks
- The Old Side and the Red Light District
- Around Herengracht
- Prinsengracht: *Noorderkerk to Weesperplein*
- Markets and the Amstel

Harbours and the Sea
- Oosterdok: *The East Harbour*
- Westelijk Eilanden: *The Western Islands*
- Scheveningen
- Rotterdam 1: *Weena to the Maas*

Parks and Gardens
- The Rijksmuseum and the Vondelpark
- The Plantage and the Artis Zoo
- The Keukenhof
- Rotterdam 2: *Parks and museums*

Shopping and Markets
- The Jordaan
- The Hague 2: *Art, antiques and parks*
- Nieuwmarkt to Waterlooplein: *The Jewish Quarter*/The Plantage and the Artis Zoo
- Markets and the Amstel/The Plantage and the Artis Zoo
- Rotterdam 1/Rotterdam 2
- Haarlem 1/Haarlem 2

Architecture and Historic Buildings
- The Dam: *Old Amsterdam*
- Around Herengracht
- The Hague 1: *Historic Buildings*
- Rotterdam 1: *Weena to the Maas*
- Haarlem 1/Haarlem 2
- Delft
- Gouda
- Utrecht
- Leiden 2: *City almshouses*

Circular Walks
- The Dam: *Old Amsterdam*
- The Old Side and the Red Light District
- The Rijksmuseum and the Vondelpark
- The Plantage and the Artis Zoo
- Oosterdok: *The East Harbour*
- Westelijk Eilanden: *The Western Islands*
- The Hague 1: *Historic buildings*
- Scheveningen
- Rotterdam 1/Rotterdam 2
- Haarlem 1: *The Grote Markt and Flemish Haarlem*
- Haarlem 2: *Museums and monuments*
- Delft
- Gouda
- Utrecht
- Leiden 1: *Young Rembrandt*
- Leiden 2: *City almshouses*
- Leiden 3: *Museums*
- The Keukenhof

Connecting Walks
- Old Side and the Red Light District/Nieuwmarkt to Waterlooplein: *The Jewish Quarter*

WALKS IN ORDER OF LENGTH

(Lengths given are approximate.)

3–3.5km (around 2 miles)

- The Dam: *Old Amsterdam*
- The Old Side and the Red Light District
- The Rijksmuseum and the Vondelpark
- Westelijk Eilanden: *The Western Islands*
- Rotterdam 1: *Weena to the Maas*

4–5km (2½–3 miles)

- Nieuwmarkt to Waterlooplein: *The Jewish Quarter*
- Around Herengracht
- Markets and the Amstel
- The Plantage and the Artis Zoo
- Oosterdok: *The East Harbour*
- Scheveningen
- Rotterdam 2: *Parks and museums*

- Haarlem 2: *Museums and monuments*
- Delft
- Gouda
- Leiden 3: *Museums*

6–8km (4–5 miles)

- Prinsengracht: *Noorderkerk to Weesperplein*
- The Jordaan
- The Hague 1: *Historic buildings*
- The Hague 2: *Art, antiques and parks*
- Haarlem 1: *The Grote Markt and Flemish Haarlem*
- Utrecht
- Leiden 1: *Young Rembrandt*
- Leiden 2: *City almshouses*
- The Keukenhof

AMSTERDAM

Amsterdam stands on the estuary of the River Ij, close to its mouth on the landlocked Ijsselmeer (formerly known as the Zuiderzee) and about 20km (12 miles) from the North Sea coast. Throughout its 800-year history, Amsterdam has combined a hard-headed approach to commerce and business with a remarkable willingness to experiment with new ideas, from the rationalism of Erasmus and the revolutionary Protestantism of Luther, through the republicanism of the 17th century to, more recently, the famously liberal approach to the problems of drug abuse and commercial sex.

Modern Amsterdam benefits from the legacy of its prosperous past. The city's 16th- and 17th-century merchant princes used their wealth to build gracious homes which still line the canal, and. they were the patrons of a generation of Europe's greatest painters, giving impetus to an artistic tradition which makes Amsterdam one of Europe's great centres of the visual arts today.

The Dam: Old Amsterdam

This circular walk introduces you to central Amsterdam, taking you from the city's original waterfront into its historic heart.

Start/finish: Stationsplein Metro, served by all trams
Length: 3km (2 miles)
Time: 2hr
Refreshments: Cafés, restaurants and taverns at frequent intervals along the way
Which day: Any day
To visit:
- Nieuwe Kerk: daily 11.00–17.00
- Koninklijk Paleis (Royal Palace): September–May Tuesday–Thursday 13.00–16.00, June–August daily 12.30–17.00
- Madame Tussaud Scenerama: July–August daily 09.30–21.30, September–June daily 10.00–17.30
- Oude Kerk: Monday–Saturday 11.00–17.00, tower open June–September weekdays and Saturdays 1400–1600
- Museum Amstelkring: Monday–Friday 10.00–17.00, Saturday and Sunday 11.00–17.00
- Geels & Co. Koffie en Theemuseum: Tuesday, Friday and Saturday 14.00–17.00

Amsterdam Centraal Station is a fitting gateway to the city. Built in 1882–89, at the height of the steam age, it was designed by P.J.H. Cuypers (1827–1921), who also designed the Rijksmuseum (see page 60). Both buildings are now regarded as important parts of the city's architectural heritage, but when they were built Cuypers' then innovative designs were harshly criticized. The station, built on a man-made island resting on 26,000 wooden piles, shuts central Amsterdam off from the open waters of the Ij basin. Its towered central block is elaborately turreted and ornamented.

Leaving the grandiose station façade behind you, cross the Open Haven canal dock to Prins Hendrikkade – the long boulevard which forms the northern boundary of central Amsterdam – at its junction with Martelaarsgracht. On the corner, the Café Karpershoek, a traditional 'brown tavern', claims to be the oldest in Amsterdam. About 100m (110yd) south, fork left onto Nieuwezijds Voorburgwal. The buildings which line it are a mixture of old and new. Nos. 29 and 31 lean at precarious angles.

Look above the door of no. 29 for the typical gablestone, this one depicting the Holy Family on their flight from Egypt. In earlier times, when many city-folk were

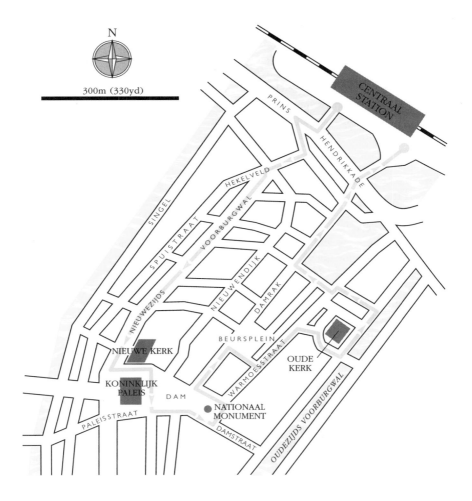

illiterate, these gablestones served as address markers, frequently representing the householder's trade or being a riddle or pun on the family name. The gablestones are protected by law as part of Amsterdam's heritage; when a building is demolished or restored, its gablestone is salvaged to be mounted on the new façade. (Look out for them around the city; the tradition is carried on, especially in the bohemian Jordaan neighbourhood – see page 53 – where many people have commissioned witty modern stones for their new homes.) The tiled gablestone of the Hotel Sofitel, at no. 65, depicts two kneeling giants and the triple-cross coat-of-arms of the city. A few doors down, at no. 75, is 't Makelaers Comtoir, a cream and red extravagance of brick arches in ascending tiers, built in 1633.

Carry on down Nieuwezijds Voorburgwal. On the west (right-hand) side of the street are two conspicuous buildings: the Hotel and Restaurant de Poort van Cleve, on the site of one of Amsterdam's oldest grand hostelries, and next to it the great Magna Plaza shopping centre. This palatial building, with its elaborate bell-tower, turrets, onion-domes and gargoyles, looks more like a fairy-tale palace. In fact, built in 1908 in Dutch Renaissance style, it was originally the city's main post office. The creamy stone colonnades and galleries of its interior are richly adorned with shields, crests and – again – gargoyles, and are now lined with expensive up-market designer-name shops.

Back on the east side of Nieuwezijds Voorburgwal, walk down a small side-street, Mozes en Aaronstraat, which leads to the Dam. On your left, occupying most of the block, is the Nieuwe Kerk. It dates from the late 15th century but was several times damaged by fire and subsequently restored; its vaulted interior dates from the 17th century. The delicately carved Baroque pulpit and stained-glass windows are worth a close look. The kings and queens of the Netherlands are crowned here; the church also presents a frequently changing programme of cultural exhibitions. Among the famous Amsterdammers buried here is Joost van den Vondel (1587–1679), regarded as the greatest Dutch poet and playwright. He lived to be 92 – a remarkable achievement in itself, in the 17th century. His epitaph reads:

Hier ligt Vondel zonder Rouw
Hij is gestorven van de kou

which can be somewhat freely translated as:

Here lies Vondel, whom none rue,
Carried off by a nasty 'flu

The earliest village

Mozes en Aaronstraat now opens onto the Dam, the site of the first settlement. It grew up around the castle built by Gijsbrecht, first Lord of Amstel, in the 12th century. Under Gijsbrecht and his successors the river was dammed and its waters diverted, and the settlement took the name Aemstelle Dam – the dam on the Amstel. Today this open space is used for ceremonies related to the royal family, for social gatherings and for demonstrations aimed at drawing attention to a broad spectrum of political and human-rights causes. In summer, street performers entertain sightseers with mime, juggling, fire-eating, music and clowning. The 'square' is in fact an irregular rectangle, bisected by the Damrak and Rokin traffic arteries running roughly north–south through the city-centre.

From Town Hall to Royal Palace

The entire west end of the square is occupied by the massive Koninklijk Paleis (Royal Palace), built in 1648–55 at the height of the Dutch Republic's Golden Age. The Baroque–Classical exterior, designed by Jacob van Campen (1595–1657), is more sober and less regal than you might expect, perhaps because it lacks a grand ceremonial doorway: its builders intended it to be easily defended against rebellious mobs. The façade is crowned by an elaborately carved pediment decorated with unicorns and other allegorical creatures. On the roof, overlooking the Dam, stand statues of the Virtues – Peace, Prudence and Justice – while looking down from the back of the building is Atlas, bearing a great green globe and flanked by Temperance and Vigilance. Above everything is a huge cupola crowned by a galleon weathervane.

Built as the city's town hall – its predecessor was destroyed by fire – the palace became a royal residence only in 1808, when Louis Bonaparte, foisted onto the Dutch as king by his brother Napoleon, moved in. On his departure – leaving behind some fine French Empire furniture – it became the Amsterdam residence of the royal house of Orange, though it remained the property of the city until it was sold to the crown in 1935.

The palatial interior is far more exciting. The great halls are lavishly furnished and decorated. On the ground floor, Biblical allegories in stone decorate the Marble Tribunal, once the city's main courtroom; condemned prisoners were taken from here to be hanged on a public scaffold on the Dam. Each upper-floor room housed a different department of the city administration, and they are adorned with works of art appropriate to their function, mainly sculpture and painting inspired by Biblical and Classical mythology.

The most impressive of all is the grand Burgerzaal (Citizens' Hall). Louis Bonaparte used it as his throne room. Its interior is clad almost entirely in marble, and its marvellous floor is inlaid with maps of the world; above stands a magnificently muscled Atlas bearing a starry globe. The galleries surrounding the hall and leading to the adjoining rooms are decorated with dynamic canvases of early Dutch history by the masters Govaert Flinck (1615–1660), Jakob Jordaens (1593–1678), Jan Lievens (1607–1674) and Jurgen Ovens (1623–1678). Rembrandt is conspicuous by his absence: he was out of favour with the city fathers when the building was being commissioned. The oligarchs favoured painters who would flatter their conception of themselves as statesmen in the mould of Periclean Athens or Republican Rome; Rembrandt's sly, warts-and-all style was deemed to be unacceptable.

Before leaving the palace, visit the ten-minute slide show on historic Amsterdam and check out the relief map of the medieval city, displayed on the ground floor.

Waxworks, commemoration and money

Exit the palace, turn right and cut across the Dam to its south side. At no. 20 you will find the Madame Tussaud Scenerama, where special effects re-create the sounds and sights (though fortunately not the smells) of three centuries ago.

Walk east over the square to your next landmark, the Nationaal Monument (National Monument), commemorating the Dutch victims of World War II. Reliefs on the sides of the 22m (72ft) column and its surrounding walls, sculpted by J.W.

Radeler, symbolize war, peace and resistance. The monument was consecrated on 4 May 1956, eleven years to the day after the liberation of the city by Canadian and British troops.

Cross to the north side of the Dam, turn left along it, then turn right onto the Damrak. Keep to the east side of the street as you head north; the grand façade of the Centraal Station is visible at the end of this long, straight boulevard. Head towards it until, about 100m (110yd) north of the Dam, you reach the Beursplein, dominated on its north and east sides by the buildings of the Beurs (Exchange) van Berlage and the Effectenbeurs.

Built in 1903 and named after its architect, Hendrick Petrus Berlage (1856–1934) – a pupil of Cuypers – the Beurs prefigures many of the tenets of modern architecture. Its lines are stripped of decoration to the point of sterility, but the brick building is saved from drabness by its fine proportions. Its clock tower bears the motto Beidt uw tijd (Bide your time) – appropriate enough, considering that Berlage was only a runner-up in the first competition to appoint an architect for the building. He won the second contest, mounted after the winner of the first was found to have pirated his design from another building.

The Beurs is now a concert hall, and its commercial activities have been transferred to the neighbouring Effectenbeurs (Commodities Exchange), on the east side of the square. Next to the simple façade of the Beurs, this Neoclassical building appears a riot of decoration. Its second-floor balcony is supported by four larger-then-life elephant heads, and the top-floor brickwork is picked out in bright colours. A marble portico surrounds three massive black iron-bound doors.

The oldest street and the oldest church

Cut down the south side of the Effectenbeurs, following the narrow Papenbrugsteeg onto Warmoesstraat, the oldest street in the city. Tenants through the ages have included the Duke of Alva, the Spanish tyrant, in 1574; the poet Vondel, a century or so later; the Mozarts (father and son) in 1766; and Karl Marx (1818–1883), in exile from Germany, in the 1850s. These days it shows its age: a handful of tatty pornographers and sleazy bars are interspersed with everyday shops; one of the more amusing is the Condomerie het Gulden Vlies, facing you as you leave Papenbrug-steeg, which sells condoms in every conceivable shape, size, colour and even flavour. The window display is an eye-opener even to the least shockable.

Turn left up Warmoesstraat and go almost immediately right onto St Annenstraat, a narrow street which after only 50m (55yd) brings you out on the west bank of the Oudezijds Voorburgwal canal. Another left turn and a further 50m (55yd) walk bring you to the Oude Kerk, the oldest church – and indeed one of the oldest buildings – in Amsterdam. Just before you get to the church you pass one of the most vividly painted of Amsterdam's famous coffee shops. The Bulldog boasts it has been in business since 1975, and its psychedelic interior decoration takes you back to the golden age of hippiedom. The fragrant fumes drifting from within are not just from the coffee.

Archaeological work indicates that a small church existed on this canal-side site as early as the 13th century. The Gothic church tower dates from 1306, but most of the rest of this solid, massive-seeming brick building, dwarfing the houses which surround it, was added or rebuilt in the 16th century. The 65m (220ft) wooden steeple was added in 1566, and the interior has been altered so often over almost seven centuries that its original builders would certainly not recognize it. The splendid altars of its Roman Catholic era were destroyed during the Reformation, when it became a Protestant place of worship, but in the Chapel of Our Lady survive three stained-glass windows dating from 1555. Designed by Pieter Aertzoon (c.1508–1579), these show scenes from the Nativity and the Annunciation. Among the people buried in the church is Rembrandt's wife, Saskia, whose tomb is on the north side of the church.

A hidden church

Leaving the church, turn left and walk along the Oudezijds Voorburgwal canal, past the incongruous displays of scantily clad female flesh in the first windows of the Red Light District, to the Museum Amstelkring at Oudezijds Voorburgwal 40. The museum is housed in a 17th-century merchant's home, and each room is authentically furnished; the parlour is, to the last detail, in the style of the 18th century. Climb the increasingly cramped stairs – pausing to glance into the cosy but cramped bedrooms with their tiny box beds – to discover the museum's cunningly concealed surprise. At the top of the smallest, ladder-like stair you step not into a dusty attic, but into a spacious and richly decorated place of worship.

The attic of the house was the last of Amsterdam's schuilkerks, or clandestine churches. It was known as Ons Lieve Heer op de Solder (Our Dear Lord in the Attic). In post-Reformation Amsterdam, Catholic masses were outlawed; but, once the first blaze of Protestant fervour had faded, they were tolerated so long as they were held in private.

From the Amstelkring Museum, retrace your steps for some 100m (110yd) to the Niezel Bridge, which crosses the canal to your left. Turn right, into Oude Lange Niezel. Continue along this street to the corner of Warmoesstraat to visit the Geels & Co. Koffie en Theemuseum (Coffee and Tea Museum) at no. 67. Geels, one of the city's longest-established importers, sells the finest coffee in Amsterdam.

From here, cross Warmoesstraat to emerge after about 200m (220yd) on the Damrak, an inner harbour where you can see Amsterdam's fleet of sleek white canal cruisers at their moorings. Turn right and walk along its banks back to Amsterdam Centraal Station, which you can see a few hundred metres away across the waters of the Open Haven.

The Old Side and the Red Light District

The Old Side is the oldest continuously inhabited part of the city. A narrow finger of land, nowhere more than a couple of hundred metres wide and about 1.5km (1 mile) in length, it is bounded by the waters of the Oudezijds Voorburgwal ('inside the city wall') and Oudezijds Achterburgwal ('outside the city wall') canals. It presents some of Amsterdam's oddest contrasts. At its upper end, and spilling over to the other side of the Oudezijds Voorburgwal, are the fleshpots of the city's famous Red Light District, from which near-naked or provocatively clad women and transvestites beckon passers-by, but also, overlooking all this, are some of Amsterdam's most prominent churches. During daytime the sex shops, massage parlours and go-go bars look just sad and seedy; everyday life goes on around them, the ordinary inhabitants of the Old Side seemingly oblivious to the ubiquitous sleaze. At night, the glow of coloured neon lends the whole scene a somewhat spurious air of glamour and excitement.

This walk begins at the Damrak and takes you around the Old Side, crossing the Oudezijds Achterburgwal to visit a cluster of historic buildings, then returns through Amsterdam's Chinatown.

Start:	Outside the Beurs van Berlage, at the corner of Oude Lange Niezel and Damrak; trams 4, 9, 16, 24, 25
Finish:	Stationsplein Metro, served by all trams
Length:	3.2km (2 miles)
Time:	1hr
Refreshments:	This is an expensive area, and most bars are more or less tacky. If you plan to view the district at night, there are lots of Asian restaurants – not just Chinese, but Thai, Indonesian and Indian – along the upper end of Zeedijk; most do not open for lunch. For daytime walkers, there are pleasant café-bars along the west and north sides of the Nieuwmarkt, where, too, a row of stalls sells typical Dutch snacks like pickled herring.
Which day:	Any day
To visit:	● Hanky Panky Tattooing Museum and House of Pain: irregular hours ● Cannabis Museum: daily 10.00–18.00

Leaving the busy traffic of the Damrak behind you, walk southeast along Oude Lange Niezel; the increasing density of suggestively named bars, curtained shop windows and pink neon light indicates you are on the fringe of the Red Light District. Amsterdam has no inhibitions about what kind of pictorial material may be openly displayed, and some of the video packages, books and even postcards in shop windows are extremely anatomically explicit. Crossing the bridge from Oude Lange

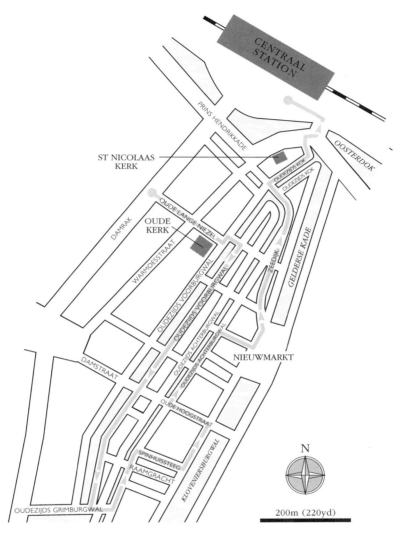

Niezel to Korte Niezel, on the Old Side, you have a view of two of Amsterdam's imposing churches. The roofs and domes of the St Nicolaas Kerk, a few hundred metres to the north, and the bell-tower of the Oude Kerk, 50m (55yd) south of the bridge, look tolerantly down on the fleshpots. From the bridge you have a fine view also of some of the handsome 17th- and 18th-century homes on the other side of the canal. (All over Amsterdam, you often find these tall, narrow canal-side townhouses are best viewed from the opposite bank, where it is easier to see the richly decorated gables that give each house such an individual air.) No. 14 Oudezijds Voorburgwal, with its six-stepped gable and row after row of red-shuttered windows, looks like a child's advent calendar or a multi-occupancy cuckoo clock. No. 19, opposite the Amstelkring Museum, has what is known as a 'neck-gable', with two delightful plunging dolphins in carved stone, one on each side. Gable decorations were often inspired by the owner's source of wealth, and many have maritime themes. A stone plaque indicates that no. 187 was built in 1656.

Sleazy streets

Turning right down Oudezijds Voorburgwal and entering the Old Side, you quickly notice a change in the atmosphere and in the streetlife; gaggles of nervous tourists try to appear blasé as they are beckoned by ladies of the night. People of uncertain gender, clad in gold lamé, rub shoulders with shaven-headed men clad head-to-foot in black leather, perhaps on their way to one of the discos advertising 'strict leather dress code' — or to no. 141 Oudezijds Voorburgwal, where a gaudily painted cellar door advertises one of Amsterdam's kinkier institutions: the Hanky Panky Tattooing Museum and House of Pain. Amsterdam's tattoo parlours are world-famous among cognoscenti, and Hanky Panky owner Henk Schiffmacher is organizer of the city's annual Tattoo Convention, held each April. The museum is not for the weak of stomach or tender of heart, as it illustrates quite how far some people are prepared to go just to look different; one of the prize exhibits is 'Captain Ahab's arm', the preserved forearm skin of a tattooed sailor, decorated with pictures of ships, whales and women.

At no. 187 — opposite the Oude Kerk — pause to note the rich façade of the so-called House of Pillars. The four brick pilasters of the lowest row are Tuscan in style, the next four Ionic and the top two Corinthian. Around these are stylized clusters of fruit and geometric shapes and, capping the lot, on either side of the neck-gable, are the figures of an Indian and an African reclining on bales and stacks of trade goods; this may indicate that the merchant who commissioned the house in 1663 was a trader in slaves as well as in tobacco and other goods.

Return to respectability

Sex dominates this side of the Oudezijds Voorburgwal — in the form of strip shows, video stores, cinemas and massage parlours — until you cross Prinsenhofstraat, when the neighbourhood suddenly buttons itself up and turns respectable. Close to the end of the canal, the St Agnieten Museum is housed in a 15th-century convent; its collection of photographs, prints and documents connected with the University of Amsterdam, whose buildings cluster on the other side of the canal, is not likely to interest the casual visitor.

Cross the canal by the small bridge (which connects with Enge Lombardsteeg) for a glimpse of another historic building. The Stadsbank van Lening started life as a

Plate 1: *The portico of the Royal Palace, on the Dam square (see the Dam: Old Amsterdam walk, page 18).*

Plate 2: *The Dam has been a counter-culture meeting-place since the 1960s and still attracts young travellers (see the Dam: Old Amsterdam walk, page 18).*

Plate 3: *Zeedijk crosses Oudezijds Achterburgwal, with the St Nicolaas Kerk in the background (see the Old Side and the Red Light District walk, page 27).*

Plate 4: The Old Side and its red light district display a blend of domesticity, eccentricity and sleaze (see the Old Side and the Red Light District walk, page 24).

Plate 5: The Montelbaanstoren, overlooking the Oude Schans, was a favourite subject of Rembrandt's. The artist lived within sight of the tower (see the Nieuwmarkt to Waterlooplein: The Jewish Quarter walk, page 30).

Plate 6: The tall houses along the Herengracht were built by old Amsterdam's wealthiest merchants (see the Around Herengracht walk, page 36).

Plate 7: Skimming along here beside the Spiegelgracht, bicycles are a popular and practical way of getting around the city (see the Prinsengracht: Nooderkerk to Weesperplein walk, page 43).

Plate 8: The Bloemenmarkt, on the banks of the Singel, is one of Amsterdam's most colourful sights (see the Markets and the Amstel walk, page 50).

storehouse for peat, then one of the city's vital fuels (it was brought in by barge from the surrounding boglands). In 1614 it became the municipal loan office, a city-operated pawnbroker where merchants short of ready cash to finance a hot deal could at short notice raise capital against the family assets.

Where three canals meet

Retrace your steps to the other side of the canal, turning right, then left at the tip of the Old Side onto Grimburgwal. You find yourself on a complicated little corner where three canals – Oudezijds Voorburgwal, Oudezijds Achterburgwal and Oudezijds Grimburgwal – meet. Aptly, the building which occupies the narrowest end of this block of buildings has the name Huis op de Drie Grachten (House on the Three Canals); surprisingly, in a city filled with canals, no other house has this distinction. It is a striking brick building with four-tiered step-gables at each end and in the centre of its frontal façade – so that one step-gable faces each of the three canals – and pretty white-framed leaded windows set in decorative arches. Within is an antiquarian library, although its contents are really of interest only to specialists; outside, ranks of student bicycles are tethered to the bridge railings.

Cross here to the east side of the Oudezijds Achterburgwal and, turning left again, follow the canal to Spinhuissteeg, noting as you pass the pleasingly higgledy-piggledy façade of no. 191 Oudezijds Achterburgwal, where a sign advertises 'old bikes for new'; inside, this bicycle-maker's shop is a clutter of elderly frames and wheels and boxes of gears and chains awaiting recycling – hopefully before the building topples into the canal, as it looks ready to do at any time.

The Spinhuis, on your left, was a 16th-century attempt to rehabilitate the prostitutes of what was even then Amsterdam's district of ill repute. The theory was rehabilitation by locking the women up and forcing them to spin thread for the clothing of the poor! The city fathers may have naïvely hoped to turn fallen women into saved spinsters; more cynical wardens turned a blind eye to 'gentlemen visitors' in return for a well placed backhander, turning the place into just another bawdy-house. Above the door, a plaque shows what inmates who stepped out of line could expect – a flogging.

Go along Spinhuissteeg to the Kloveniersburgwal canal and turn left again. About 150m (165yd) away to the east, on the opposite side of the canal, is the prominent grey tower, with its red-and-gold clock, of the 17th-century Zuiderkerk. On your left is the giant, warehouse-like façade of the Oostindische Huis (East India House), headquarters of the Vereenigde Oostindische Compagnie (VOC; the Dutch East India Company). Built in 1642, it is a plain brick building with green double doors giving access to the storehouses on each floor that once housed the VOC's treasury of spices, silks, tea, coffee and other riches from Asia. The company was so wealthy and so powerful that its directors saw no need to waste good money embellishing the building; its only ornament is the VOC's coat-of-arms on the pediment.

The case for cannabis

At the corner of the East India House, turn left along Oude Hoogstraat to go back into the sleazy world of the Red Light District. Rejoining Oudezijds Achterburgwal, cross the canal and turn right to no. 148, which houses the Cannabis Museum – the only one of its kind in the world – with, next door, the Cannabis Connoisseurs' Club. Amsterdam has long had a liberal attitude towards soft-drug use: possession of cannabis resin (hash) or marijuana (grass) is not legal – possession of less than 30g (1oz) is technically a misdemeanour – but the authorities have long since given up prosecuting users. In many euphemistically named 'coffee shops' customers are quietly offered an 'alternative menu' from which they can choose any of a dozen types of mind-expanding smoke to enjoy at home or over a cup of coffee on the premises. As a result of this enlightened policy, cannabis users are less likely to come into contact with hard drugs; the city has much lower rates of hard-drug addiction and drug-related crime than many others with tougher regimes, and the municipal health department has recommended legalization. Despite this, in 1995 the newly elected conservative administration announced plans to reduce the number of tolerated coffee shops, blithely ignoring the considerable revenue the tourism industry gets from thousands of visitors for whom Amsterdam's main attraction is not its cultural heritage but its home-grown herbs. It is interesting that, even in the age of AIDS, the mayor's born-again puritanism does not extend to the thriving commercial sex industry of the Red Light District, arguably as great (or as little) a threat to the city's image.

The Cannabis Museum's exhibition – unashamedly tracing the positive aspects of marijuana and the cannabis plant through the ages and contrasting its medicinal, environmental and therapeutic benefits with the lethal side-effects of legal drugs such as tobacco and alcohol – is an eye-opener. The high-tech equipment and information purveyed by the Cannabis Connoisseurs' Club is startling, too. Pot-growers these days use sophisticated hydroponics, special lighting and seed-selection techniques to produce high-potency strains – just as the Netherlands' world-famous tulip cultivators mix and match to produce ever more colourful and exotic blooms.

Chinatown and the Weepers' Tower

From here, backtrack to the bridge and recross the canal, turning left on the other side to continue up Oudezijds Achterburgwal. The fourth street on your right is Bloedstraat. Turn right here to emerge on the Nieuwmarkt. Here you can either pause for refreshment and a short rest before beginning the Nieuwmarkt to Waterlooplein walk (see page 28) or turn left at the north corner of the square onto Zeedijk and finish this walk with a stroll through what is sometimes known as Amsterdam's Chinatown.

In fact, this part of the city reflects every facet of the Netherlands' colonial heritage. Faces in the street may come from the former Dutch Indies (now Indonesia), the former Dutch Guyana (now Surinam) or from the Dutch Caribbean possessions, and as well as Chinese stores and restaurants there are Indonesian, Thai, Indian and lots of other ethnic restaurants. Zeedijk – originally the 'sea wall' of the old city – is now well inland (at least by Amsterdam standards) and winds its way towards the junction of Oudezijds Achterburgwal and Oudezijds Voorburgwal, on your left.

The Zeedijk now crosses another waterway, the narrow Oudezijds Kok, by an arched bridge. The Oudezijds Kok has doors for loading and unloading opening right onto the canal; turn right along it and walk towards the Oosterdok, pausing by the Schreierstoren, the last surviving bastion of the earliest city defences. It was named the Weepers' Tower because wives and sweethearts gathered here when their menfolk went to sea. They would be away for years at a time, and many never returned. A gablestone on the tower shows the wailing womenfolk.

Among the luckier mariners was Henry Hudson (*c*.1550–1611), who set off from here in 1609 seeking a westward route to the riches of Asia – the fabled Northwest Passage. Hudson was under contract to the Dutch East India Company. His exploration of the North American coast convinced the Dutch that what they had hoped was a passage to the Pacific was no more than a river, but it paved the way for Dutch settlement of Nieuw Amsterdam – now New York – and the land around what is still known as the Hudson River. A plaque commemorates his voyage.

St Nicolaas Kerk

Turn right along Oudezijds Kolk, and then left as Oudezijds Kolk meets Prins Hendrikkade. The final landmark on this walk is the St Nicolaas Kerk (St Nicholas Church), which you first saw on your right immediately after you passed the junction of the two canals. In an overwhelmingly Protestant city, this is one of the few prominent Catholic churches. Despite its neo-Renaissance architecture, it is a clumsy, looming building, and neither its gloomy interior nor its grimy exterior offer much spiritual uplift. It was built much later than the other principal churches of the city – between 1875 and 1887 – and comes into its own on the feast of St Nicholas, held on the third Saturday of November, when there is a picturesque festival gathering. St Nicholas, the patron saint of merchants and fishermen, naturally has a special place in the hearts of Amsterdammers, and is also the patron saint of children. In Dutch dialect he is called Sinterklaas, but he is more widely known around the world as Santa Claus.

From here it is a short walk back to the Stationsplein, landmarked by the grand façade of the Centraal Station facing you across the Open Haven.

Nieuwmarkt to Waterlooplein: The Jewish Quarter

This walk takes you from the fringes of old Amsterdam and the Red Light District into the heart of the former Jewish district. Amsterdam's pragmatic tolerance in religious matters made it a magnet for the Sephardic Jews who fled persecution in Spain and Portugal from the beginning of the 17th century, and soon after for the Ashkenazi Jews, fleeing intolerance in Eastern Europe. While many of the Sephardic community were prosperous traders, the Ashkenazi refugees, often penniless, found it harder to gain a foothold in commercial life. Though Amsterdam was uniquely tolerant among European cities, Jews were still unable to join the tradesmen's guilds which controlled skilled labour in the city. Until the 19th century, when their position began to improve, most Amsterdam Jews lived in this eastern section of the old city, where grand synagogues and the homes of wealthy merchants contrasted with the cramped apartment dwellings of poorer working people. Amsterdam's Jewish community played a role in the city's history out of all proportion to their numbers; old Amsterdam dialect is studded with words borrowed from Hebrew and Yiddish, and lots of popular Amsterdam delicacies – including such favourites as soused herring and pickled gherkins – originated with the Jewish immigrants.

Start:	Nieuwmarkt Metro; no trams or buses
Finish:	Waterlooplein Metro; trams 9, 14
Length:	4km (2½ miles)
Time:	2hr
Refreshments:	Cafés, bars and stalls in the Neuwmarkt, within the Stopera and around St Antonies Sluis
Which day:	Any day, but Saturday is best for Waterlooplein Fleamarket; note that the Nieuwmarkt antique market is open Sundays in spring and summer only
To visit:	● Nieuwmarkt Antique Market: March–September Sunday 10.00–16.00
	● Zuiderkerk: Monday–Wednesday and Friday 12.00–17.00, Thursday 12.00–20.00, tower accessible June–October Wednesday 14.00–17.00, Thursday–Friday 11.00–14.00, Saturday 11.00–16.00
	● Gassan diamonds factory: Nieuwe Uilenburgerstraat 173–175; Monday–Friday 09.00–17.00, Saturday 09.00–12.00
	● Het Rembrandthuis: Monday–Saturday 10.00–17.00, Sunday 13.00–17.00
	● Waterlooplein Fleamarket: Monday–Friday 09.00–17.00, Saturday 08.30–17.30
	● Joods Historisch Museum (Jewish Historical Museum): daily 11.00–17.00

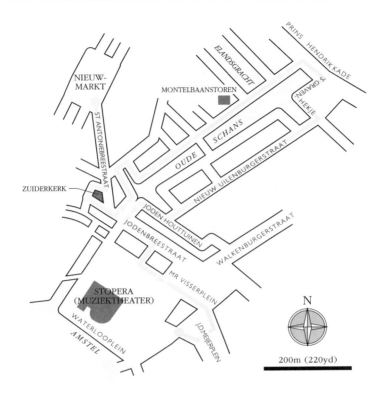

Nieuwmarkt Metro exits onto the south side of the wide and rather barren brick-cobbled square. As you pass through the station, take a look at the murals decorating its walls: they form a montage of representations of the district's past, from Rembrandt's time to the present.

The Nieuwmarkt and the streets surrounding it were the scene in the mid-1980s of one of the set-piece clashes between Amsterdam's standing army of socially conscious protesters and the municipality over plans for the Metro. Since the 1960s these confrontations have been a feature of Amsterdam politics, with local residents resisting large-scale levelling of inner-city housing in the name of development. Most visitors will instinctively sympathize with the protesters. Inner Amsterdam is livelier and safer than the centres of most big cities precisely because it has not been turned into a ghetto of office blocks.

The battle for the Nieuwmarkt ended in a draw. The district is no longer the quiet neighbourhood of cheap working-class accommodation it once was, but neither has the arrival of the Metro turned it – as the protesters feared – into a yuppie heaven where accommodation would be too expensive for ordinary Amsterdammers.

When there is no market in progress the Nieuwmarkt square is unexciting, but the stout castle-like building close to its northern corner is worth a look. This is the St Antoniespoort (St Anthony's Gate), also known as the Waag (the weigh-gate). Built in 1488, the red brick tower is among the few remnants of the early city fortifications. It originally guarded a gate piercing the walls, but a century later Amsterdam had overspilled its old defences and the redundant gate-tower was turned into a weighing place for products from the nearby foundry, which cast cannon and anchors for the ever-expanding Dutch fleet. It was also the headquarters of the city guilds, as well as a courtroom and place of execution. During this century it has housed archives, guilds and museums, but at present it is not in use.

An inspiring spire

Leave the Nieuwmarkt by St Antoniebreestraat, off the southern corner, and walk briskly down this modern shopping street to turn right, via a narrow arched gateway between nos. 130 and 132, into Zuiderkerkhof. The Zuiderkerk (South Church), in the middle of this small square, is landmarked by its graceful spire and clock tower, embellished with red and gold dials. Designed in 1603 by Hendrik de Keyser (1565–1621), the Zuiderkerk was the city's first post-Reformation Protestant church, and its graceful spire is claimed to have inspired Sir Christopher Wren (1632–1723), architect of St Paul's Cathedral and other historic London churches.

Go back through the Zuiderkerk gateway and turn right. At no. 69 St Antoniebreestraat, the De Pinto House was built in Italian Renaissance style by Isaac de Pinto, head of a Jewish dynasty who fled Spanish-ruled Antwerp in 1680. The building is now used as a public library. Its lovely painted ceiling is well worth a quick look. Continue to the street's opening onto the waterfront at St Antonies Sluis.

A leaning tower

Turn left here to walk up the northwest side of the Oude Schans, a wide waterway leading off to the Oosterdok. Houseboats are scattered along its banks, and in spring coots and great-crested grebes build floating nests of reeds and trash along the banks. Your next outstanding landmark is the Montelbaanstoren (Montelbaan Tower), built as a defensive tower in 1512 and prettified a century later by Hendrik de Keyser (1565–1621), who endowed it with one of his noted steeples above an eight-sided upper section. This made it top-heavy, and it began to lean precariously canalwards; the burghers, seeing no benefit in having a rival to the Leaning Tower of Pisa, had it hauled upright again and reinforced its foundations. Rembrandt, who lived not far away at the other end of the canal, made a number of drawings and etchings of the tower, and it was a rendezvous for Jewish refugees from Spain and Portugal. On the house opposite the tower, elegant coloured gablestones depict a Roman emperor and empress, a visual pun on the householder's family name, de Keyser (Caesar).

Walk on up the Oude Schans, crossing the bridge at the junction of this canal with, coming from your left, Elandsgracht, which is a favourite houseboat mooring. Continue to the busy traffic of Prins Hendrikkade. Turn right, crossing the mouth of the Oude Schans, and right again onto 's Gravenhekje. The warehouses on the corner belonged to the Dutch West India company, whose coat-of-arms adorns the pediment. Follow the canal bank around to the left until you reach the Peperbrug (Pepper Bridge). Turn right to cross this onto Nieuw Uilenburgerstraat. The bridge, and the adjoining Peperstraat, get their name from the warehouses here that used to store the Dutch East India Company's prized spice stocks. Immediately after the bridge, on the left side of Nieuw Uilenburgerstraat, is a row of warehouses (now converted into apartments) that each bear the name of one of the German river-ports – Cologne, Coblenz, Mainz, Frankfurt, Bonn and Mannheim – whose trade passed through the Amsterdam entrepôt. An elaborate relief on each gable depicts the waterfront of the relevant city.

City of diamonds

Walk down Nieuw Uilenburgerstraat to its southern end. On your left, just before the junction with Uilenburgersteeg, is the Gassan diamonds factory. Built in 1879 by the Boas family, it is open to the public, with daily tours and demonstrations of diamond cutting and polishing.

Amsterdam became Europe's pre-eminent diamond broking and cutting centre as a result of a combination of religious tolerance and intolerance. As we have seen, Jews arriving in the city from Spanish lands were not persecuted, and were permitted to worship openly – the Great Synagogue, further along this walk, is the oldest synagogue in Western Europe – but they did suffer discrimination and were excluded from the city guilds and professions. Many of the Sephardic Jews who arrived in Amsterdam from Spanish-held Antwerp in the early 17th century were diamond dealers with Portuguese connections. They dealt in raw diamonds, recruiting cutters and polishers from the Jewish community. Barred from other trades, Jewish workers came to excel in this new skill. In the 19th century the diamond trade expanded from a cottage industry into a fully industrialized process. Steam-powered tools were introduced in 1845, and the discovery of vast diamond fields in South Africa in 1869 led to a boom. Amsterdam remained the diamond capital of the world until World War II, when most of the city's Jewish workers were deported and murdered by the German occupiers. Ironically, post-war Antwerp won back leadership of the world diamond market it had lost 350 years earlier.

Cross the canal and walk down Uilenburgersteeg to Jodenbreestraat, once the bustling heart of Jewish Amsterdam, and turn right. Much of Jodenbreestraat's character has been destroyed over the past few decades, first by the Nazi Holocaust and later by the demolition of its entire north side to make way for the dull modern block, built in 1965, which now occupies the site. A century ago the street was a

31

colourful maze of slum apartments and alleys where the poorest Jewish families lived, often ten to a room.

Rembrandt at home

In 1639, Rembrandt van Rijn bought the red-shuttered house at 4–6 Jodenbreestraat, close to the St Antonies Sluis. He was by then an established painter, and had further secured his creature comforts by marrying a wealthy heiress, Saskia van Uylenburgh (*c.*1612–1642). The Jewish quarter provided him with many of his models, especially when he was painting the Biblical themes he loved. Rembrandt lived here for almost 20 years, but in later life he fell on hard times. His work was no longer fashionable, and in 1656 he was declared bankrupt, and the house sold. The Rembrandthuis is now a museum, with 250 of his etchings on show – too many to take in at one gulp.

Turn left as you come out of the Rembrandthuis and right from Jodenbreestraat into Waterlooplein. This flat area on the banks of the River Amstel is an artificial island, raised above flood-level from a swampy sandbank in the late 16th century. Soon after, Jewish immigrants from Portugal and the East began to settle here. The better-off Portuguese Sephardim, who were among the first arrivals, could afford to build salubrious homes overlooking the Amstel; the poorer Ashkenazi exiles from Eastern Europe crammed into the rookeries inland, and the district became a densely populated, three-dimensional labyrinth of alleys and tenements. It was not until the late 19th century that the district took a turn for the better. Two canals leading off the Amstel were filled in, creating a large open space, and the stallholders who had peddled their goods in the cramped alleys were relocated to this new site. In the post-war years the Jewish quarter was a ghost town in every sense of the word; of its 80,000 people, only about 5000 survived the Nazi pogroms.

The daily market held here, though colourful enough, is a mere shadow of the original fleamarket. Its clutter of stalls, selling neo-hippie gear, cheap jewellery, junk, old clothes and perhaps even the occasional genuine antique, is duplicated in similar markets all over Europe.

An open secret

Turn left and walk through the market, passing the portico of the Mozes en Aaron-kerk (Moses and Aaron Church), built in 1841 on the site of one of Amsterdam's 'secret' Catholic churches (see page 21). Like present-day 'coffee shops', the clandestine churches were very much an open secret. The original Mozes en Aaronkerk, built in 1686 – the predecessor of the one now facing you – had room for 2000 worshippers, who could hardly have entered it unnoticed.

The complex of modern buildings which occupies the site between the Waterloo-plein and the River Amstel is the Muziektheater. Familiarly known as the Stopera, it houses the National Ballet, the Netherlands Dance Theatre, the Netherlands Opera and the new Stadhuis (Town Hall). There are cafés and restaurants within the complex, and it is not a bad place for refreshment on a winter or spring day, when the Waterlooplein can be chilly and windswept.

Cross Mr Visserplein, which is named for Louis Ernst Visser, president of the High Court when the Germans invaded the Netherlands, and honoured for his courageous defence of Jewish rights during the Nazi Occupation. In the centre of the square is the splendid Portugees Israâlitische Synagoge (Portuguese Synagogue). Built in 1675, it survived World War II and was then restored in the 1950s. Its interior, with a lofty barrel-vaulted roof, was intended by its architect, Elias Bouman — of whom very little else is known — to echo that of the Temple of Solomon. The huge space is lit by scores of arched windows and original 17th-century brass chandeliers.

Europe's earliest synagogue

Signposted off the square, the Joods Historisch Museum (Jewish Historical Museum) moved to this site in 1987 — it had been previously housed in the Waag, on Nieuwmarkt. The complex of buildings which now houses the museum comprises four Ashkenazi synagogues. (The Ashkenazi and Sephardim got along together no better than their Protestant and Catholic contemporaries — hence the demand for separate places of worship.) Less fortunate than the Portuguese synagogue during World War II, these were looted by the German occupiers.

The interiors have been painstakingly reconstructed. The oldest — the Great Synagogue, built in 1671 — is the earliest recognizable synagogue in Western Europe; until the Ashkenazi settled in tolerant Amsterdam, Jews had had to worship in clandestine synagogues. The opening of the Great Synagogue was followed by the building of the Obbene Shul (Upstairs Synagogue) in 1685, the Dritt Shul (Third Synagogue) 15 years later and the Nieuwe Shul (New Synagogue) in 1752.

Within, religious objects and artworks include the marvellous marble ark of the Great Synagogue, elaborate silverware, gorgeously embroidered prayer shawls and exhibitions of the work of Dutch Jewish painters. Upstairs, an exhibition outlines the role played by the Jewish community in the development of Amsterdam's trade and industry. A grimmer note is struck by the exhibition downstairs, showing false identification papers and ration cards used in the struggle to evade capture by the Nazis.

As you exit the synagogue, turn left and follow the narrow lane which would eventually lead you to Waterlooplein; you turn left before then to reach the Waterlooplein Metro station and the end of this walk.

Around Herengracht

This pleasant circular walk takes you round the outskirts of the early city-centre, among houses built during the latter half of the 17th century by Amsterdam's richest burghers. This is how most visitors imagine Amsterdam: tall, gabled houses along a tree-lined canal. The walk is quite a long one, and is at its most enjoyable in spring and summer.

Start:	Stationsplein Metro, which is served by all buses and trams
Finish:	Rembrandtplein (trams 4, 9, 14) or Waterlooplein Metro (trams 9, 14)
Length:	4.8km (3 miles)
Time:	2½hr
Refreshments:	Café-bars are scattered along the route and around Rembrandtplein
Which day:	Any day
To visit:	● Theatermuseum: Tuesday–Saturday 11.00–17.00
	● Bijbels Museum: Tuesday–Saturday 10.00–17.00, Sunday 13.00–17.00
	● Kattenkabinet: open for exhibitions only (tel 6265378 for details)
	● Van Loon Museum: Monday–Friday 11.00–17.00
	● Thorbeckeplein Art Market: March–October, Sunday 10.30–18.00
	● Willet–Holthuysen Museum: Monday–Friday 10.00–17.00, Saturday–Sunday 11.00–17.00

From Stationsplein, turn right along Prins Hendrikkade and keep going until you cross the Singel. Turn left and then right to come onto the north bank of Brouwersgracht. After less than 75m (80yd) you reach the small square of the Herenmarkt. On the square is the Westindische Huis, once the headquarters of the Dutch West India Company. In the 19th century the original building was transformed into an orphanage; only the 17th-century courtyard survives from its heyday.

The West India Company was formed in 1624 in the hope of finding the same sort of wealth in the west that had made the Dutch East India Company such a power in the land. However, it never became as successful as the VOC. Faring westwards across the Atlantic, it found the Spanish and Portuguese solidly in control of South America, and a series of costly wars with these rivals ate into its profits. Much of the wealth it did amass came from the slave trade between West Africa and colonies in

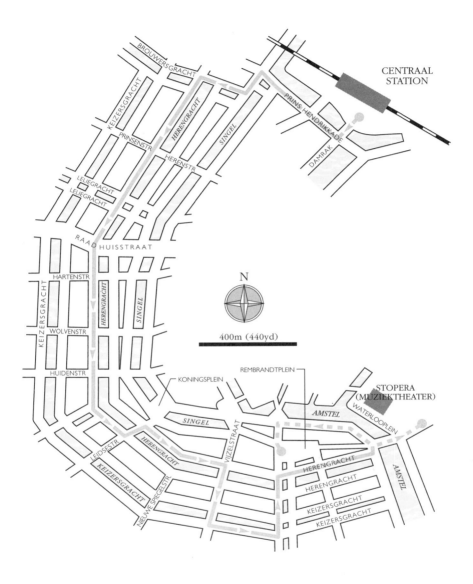

the Caribbean and South America. Following Henry Hudson's exploration of the American east coast, the Company settled colonists at Nieuw Amsterdam, on Manhattan Island, and along the Hudson River; it lost these colonies to the English in 1664.

The Gentlemen's Canal

Cross Brouwersgracht to the west bank of Herengracht – the Gentlemen's Canal – the innermost of three concentric canals that partially ring the city-centre, linking Brouwersgracht in the northwest to the Amstel in the south. These were built to provide housing land for the city's fast-growing population in the first quarter of the 17th century, when the Twelve Years' Truce with Spain (1609–21), which brought an end to decades of warfare, attracted Protestants fleeing oppression in other lands. Amsterdam's population grew from 30,000 in 1570 to 140,000 by 1640, overspilling from the city walls, which originally ran along what is now the inner side of Herengracht.

The houses of Herengracht, where the wealthiest gentry and merchants of Amsterdam's 17th-century Golden Age lived, were among the most magnificent in the city, although their magnificence is not immediately apparent from the outside. Even during its richest years, Protestant Amsterdam frowned on too lavish a public display of wealth, and the beauty of the tall canal-side mansions is in their fine proportions and craftsmanship, not in outstandingly rich decoration. Inside, however, all was luxury, with the finest of furnishings and decor. More than 400 of these houses have been listed as national monuments; sadly, maintaining them to the high standards required is too costly for most individuals, and so the majority are now banks and offices. This makes Herengracht in some ways less lively than much of the inner city, with less of the hustle and bustle of everyday life that adds to Amsterdam's charm. The buildings, however, do much to compensate for this. Many of the finest are by the architect Philips Vingboons (*c.*1608–1678), whose work was much in demand among the city's upper class.

Gable ornaments

Among Herengracht's architectural glories are its wealth of ornamented gables – there are so many of them that trying to count them all can lead to a stiff neck. Vingboons introduced the neck-gable, building the first one at no. 168, now the Theatermuseum, in 1638. Richly adorned with fruit and flower carvings, neck-gables remained popular until the late 18th century, growing steadily more elaborate. Earlier houses (from around 1600–65) had simpler step-gables of brick; elevated step-gables like those at nos. 281–283 Herengracht were an intermediate stage. Gables were status symbols. Land was always in short supply, and the city taxed householders according to the width of their frontage, so houses climbed to giddy heights. Adding another few metres to the top of your home by means of a high gable was one way to display your wealth.

Walk down the west bank of Herengracht, looking out on the other side of the canal for the converted warehouses at nos. 43–45, also known as 't Fortuin (Fortune) and Arcke Noach (Noah's Ark). Built in 1600, they are reckoned to be the oldest buildings on Herengracht.

The first stop on this walk is the Theatermuseum (Theatre Museum) at no. 168, which has a delightfully eclectic collection ranging from costumes, posters and an 18th-century miniature theatre to machines used to produce alarming sound and lighting effects. The ground-floor rooms are decorated with early 18th-century murals depicting Biblical scenes. The city burghers were fond of moral tales from the Old Testament; these were depicted by Jacob de Wit (1695–1754). Portraits of the eight Virtues and of the Fates decorate the rear parlour.

Next door, at nos. 170–172, is the delightful Bartolotti House, designed in 1615 by Hendrik de Keyser – better known for his steeples and church-towers – for a wealthy banker called Willem van de Heuvel. In contrast with the Theatermuseum's neck-gable, this has an elaborate step-gable; the face owes its present magnificence to a sensitive restoration in the 1970s.

Between the intersection with Raadhuisstraat and the junction with Leidsestraat, Herengracht is a not unattractive jumble of styles and centuries. Authentic 17th-century buildings jostle for space with 19th-century revivals and 20th-century imitations. Look out for, on the opposite side, Vingboons' pilastered stone frontage at no. 257, built in 1661 with Dorian, Ionian and Corinthian pilasters climbing to a stone neck-gable. No. 269 Herengracht dates from the same period.

At nos. 380–382 stands an unusual building, mixing US 19th-century and French château styles, but first you might like to pause for a visit to the Bijbels Museum (Bible Museum) at no. 366 Herengracht, which has a collection and exhibition dedicated to retelling the stories of the Old and New Testaments. The models of the Holy Land, Jerusalem and the Temple of Solomon are perhaps none too exciting, but the plain elegance of the simple 18th-century wooden interior is almost worth a visit on its own.

The Golden Bend

We are now approaching the most sumptuous homes on the whole Herengracht, the mansions of the so-called Golden Bend, in the crook of the canal between Koningsplein and Vijzelstraat.

By the time the wealthiest men in the city – some of them among the richest in the world – began to commission homes here in the latter part of the 17th century, considerable lavishness had entered into the style of both the houses and the materials used to build them. The owners – merchants, bankers, landowners and city burgomasters – could afford twin lots, and the extra width of these houses gives them an added air of solidity. Imported stone was used extensively in place of local brick; in the absence of the elaborate ornamentation favoured by the rich of other contemporary European cities, costly and exotic materials conveyed the notion of wealth. Don't overlook the prettiest of these houses, at no. 475, commissioned in 1668 by a merchant called Denys Nuyts and completed in 1672. Many of the exterior details, including the female figures either side of the main window, were added later in the 1730s by the then owner, Petronella van Lennep de Neufville, wealthy widow of a textile merchant.

Turn left to cross the canal by the Leidsestraat Bridge, then turn right along what is now the canal's north bank. The next stop will have a special appeal to cat-lovers, for the esoteric Kattenkabinet (Cat Museum) at no. 497 is dedicated to all things feline.

Leaving the Kattenkabinet, carry on along Herengracht until you reach the Vijzelstraat Bridge. To visit the Van Loon Museum, turn right over the bridge. The third house from the corner of Vijzelstraat and Herengracht, at no. 502, is known as the House of Columns. Built in 1672 for the director of the Dutch West India Company, Paulus Godin, it is now the official residence of the Mayor of Amsterdam. Continue along Vijzelstraat to the Museum van Loon, at no. 672 Keizersgracht, close to the corner of Vijzelstraat. Built in 1672, the house was in the possession of the van Loon family for centuries, and is filled with family heirlooms, furniture and portraits of van Loon ancestors from the 17th and 18th centuries.

Turn left as you leave the Van Loon Museum and walk along Keizersgracht – another wide, mansion-lined 17th-century canal excavated at the same time as Herengracht – until you reach the junction with Reguliersgracht, a quiet, narrow canal crossed by a string of hump-back bridges to north and south. Turn left on Reguliersgracht and follow it back up to Herengracht, turning right onto the bridge. Midway across, turn and face back down Reguliersgracht for a fine view of the six bridges over the canal. On your left, you can see six further bridges, these ones spanning Herengracht, and on your right are two more – fourteen in all (fifteen, counting the one you're standing on). Cross the bridge on your left to Thorbecke-plein, on the north side of Herengracht.

This small canal-side square is named after the liberal 19th-century politician Johan Rudolf Thorbecke, whose frock-coated statue stands looking down Reguliersgracht. Thorbecke headed a committee set up in 1848 by King William II to reform the Dutch parliamentary system. In 1849, with popular revolutions sweeping Europe, rioters in the city demanded equality for all, and a series of reforms widening the electoral franchise were pushed through. A Sunday open-air art market is held around the square.

An elegant mansion

Walk along Herengracht to the Museum Willet–Holthuysen at no. 605 for a look at what these prosperous burghers' homes were like within. The house, built in 1687 for a member of the city council, is beautifully preserved, with a rich collection of ornaments, furniture and porcelain, mostly dating from the 19th century, when this was the home of Sandra Louise Geertruida Holthuysen and her husband Abraham Willet; the couple left the house and its contents to the city to be dedicated as a museum. They were inveterate collectors of antiques and objets d'art, all of which are still there to be viewed, along with the gleaming copper and china in the

18th-century basement kitchen. The rooms are lavishly decorated in inlaid wood and lacquered panelling, and the Louis XVI dining-room, with its rich furniture and table laid for six, is particularly elegant. Abraham Willet's collection of delicate porcelain from Delft and The Hague is on display in a small, pretty room overlooking a trim garden lined with topiary. The upper-floor bedrooms are now used to display other fine pieces of glass and silverware. Abraham's taste in paintings was less reliable, for most of those on display are mediocre and some are plain bad.

Leaving the Willet–Holthuysen Museum, turn left, still following the canal; you pass a plaque recording that Rembrandt's patron, the burgomaster Jan Six, lived at no. 619; Rembrandt painted a lively portrait of Six in 1654. This house was designed for the burgomaster by Adriaen Dortsman (1625–1682) in 1667. When first built, the house was one of a row of eight designed by Dortsman. No. 623 still bears unmistakable marks of his style: its natural stone façade is divided by three narrow windows with a straight frieze and attic.

Walk on along Herengracht as far as the Blauw Brug, to your left, which crosses the wide Amstel River. Built in 1874, when cast-iron was still a relatively novel material which allowed bridge-builders a new flamboyance, its stone central piers are carved with images of boats and fish; the red granite pillars which held its streetlamps are capped by bright yellow crowns. From the middle of the bridge there is a fine view of the Amstel to the south and of the boat-filled Inner Amstel Basin to the north.

From the west end of the bridge, turn left onto Amstelstraat, which leads you to Rembrandtplein. Alternatively, cross the bridge to reach the Waterlooplein Metro station, a walk of about 400m (a quarter of a mile).

Prinsengracht: Noorderkerk to Weesperplein

This walk takes you round one of the most elegant of Amsterdam's canal rings, calling at two lively markets, two historic churches, a moving and world-famous memorial to the victims of the Holocaust, and two contrasting art museums.

Start:	Stationsplein; Metro, all buses and trams
Finish:	Weesperplein; Metro, trams 8, 7, 10
Length:	8km (5 miles)
Time:	6hr, including museums
Refreshments:	A choice selection of the city's finest and longest-established 'brown cafés' can be found on Prinsengracht, around Museumplein and within the museums
Which day:	Not Sunday; best is Saturday. Start early for the best of the Boerenmarkt and to beat the often lengthy queue at the Anne Frank House.
To visit:	● Noorderkerk: Saturdays 10.00–12.00
	● Boerenmarkt (Noordermarkt): Saturday 09.00–17.00 (produce and caged birds), Monday 09.00–17.00 (bric-à-brac)
	● Anne Frank Huis: Monday–Saturday 09.00–19.00 Sunday 10.00–19.00
	● Westerkerk: Monday–Saturday 10.00–16.00
	● Rijksmuseum Vincent van Gogh: daily 10.00–17.00
	● Stedelijk Museum: daily 11.00–17.00
	● Concertgebonw: Free lunchtime concerts, Wednesdays 12.00
	● Albert Cuypstraat Market: Monday–Saturday 09.30–17.00

Leaving Stationsplein, turn right, follow Prins Hendrikkade to where it crosses the Singel, turn left, then right along Brouwersgracht, then left again across the first bridge you reach and follow Brouwersgracht to its junction with Prinsengracht. You are now standing on Papeneiland (Papists' Island), so-called because of the Carthusian monastery which once stood here, just outside the city limits. If a canal tour boat is passing, pause to admire the skill with which the vessel is piloted through the two narrow bridges which respectively span the two canals here. The Papiermolensluis (Papermill Bridge), the one crossing Brouwersgracht, allows a clearance of barely half a metre (20in) either side.

From here, cross Prinsengracht by LeLkeresluis (Sweet Bridge, named after the pancakes once sold here). Café Papeneiland, at no. 2 Prinsengracht – on the corner by the end of the bridge – is one of several 'brown cafés' which claim the title of Amsterdam's oldest; none have firm historical proof to back up their claim. This

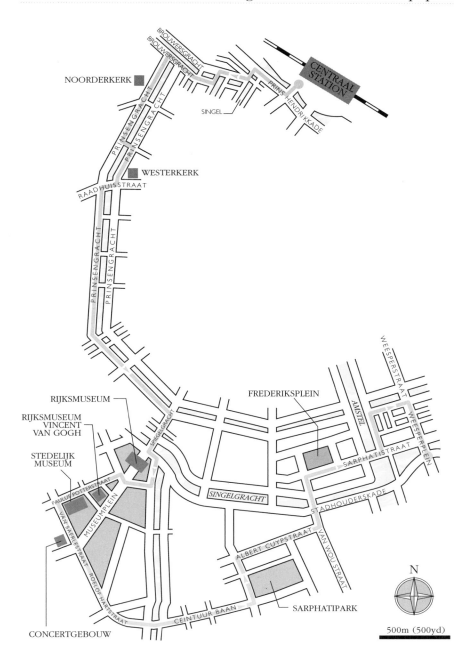

NOORDERKERK

SINGEL

WESTERKERK

RAADHUISSTRAAT

BROUWERSGRACHT
BROUWERSGRACHT

PRINSENGRACHT
PRINSENGRACHT
PRINSENGRACHT

PRINS HENDRIKKADE

CENTRAAL STATION

WEESPERSTRAAT

WEESPERPLEIN

RIJKSMUSEUM

RIJKSMUSEUM
VINCENT
VAN GOGH

STEDELIJK
MUSEUM

PAULUS POTTERSTRAAT

VAN BAERLESTRAAT

MUSEUMPLEIN

ROELOF HARTSTRAAT

CONCERTGEBOUW

CEINTUUR BAAN

SPIEGELGRACHT

SINGELGRACHT

FREDERIKSPLEIN

AMSTEL

SARPHATISTRAAT

STADHOUDERSKADE

ALBERT CUYPSTRAAT

VAN WOUSTRAAT

SARPHATIPARK

N

500m (500yd)

establishment, with its fine step-gables, dates from 1642, although it is said that a coffin-maker and undertaker sold drink here as early as 1600, presumably finding a ready market among the mourners.

The Prince's Canal

This is the outermost of three canal rings built during Amsterdam's Golden Age to house its newly wealthy merchant aristocracy. On it stand two of the four churches built in Amsterdam by the newly triumphant Protestant Reformers of the 17th century, plus a fine array of prosperous merchants' mansions of the Golden Age. From Lekkeresluis, walk southwards down the west side of the canal towards your first landmark, the looming bulk of the Noorderkerk (North Church).

Built in 1620, this church was designed by Hendrik de Keyser, architect of so many of Amsterdam's Golden Age buildings, and Hendrick Jacobszoon Staets. A solid though well proportioned building of brown brick and grey slate, this was de Keyser's last project, and represents a remarkable departure from the earlier architectural traditions of the Catholic Church. Instead of having nave, transept, choir and altar, it has the plan of a Greek cross. Four arms of equal length radiate from a centre crowned by one of de Keyser's trademark steeples. The Noorderkerk makes de Keyser's other prominent churches – the Westerkerk (see below) and the Zuiderkerk (see page 30) – seem almost frivolously pretty.

Parrots and pigeons

On a Saturday, the square between the church and the canal is lined with the stalls of the Boerenmarkt (Noordermarkt). On the north side of the square bird-fanciers gather with cages full of fancy poultry, racing pigeons, parrots, exotic finches and songbirds. The chickens and cockerels do not look too unhappy, but the cramped cages full of tiny songbirds are depressing. However, the stalls on the other side of the square present a cheering array of delicious foodstuffs. This was originally a livestock market, as you can deduce from the three gablestones on nos. 17, 18 and 19 – respectively a cow, a chicken and a sheep. Now it sells mainly organic farm produce, with locals lining up three-deep to buy tasty cheeses, freshly baked seed-flavoured bread or a dozen different kinds of exotic wild fungus.

Your next landmark, already in sight, is another of de Keyser's churches. The Westerkerk (West Church), its tower capped by a blue orb and crown and a gilded weathercock, is perhaps the prettiest of the four 17th-century churches built at the four compass points around the city-centre. Before reaching it, cross the canal and join the queue at no. 263 Prinsengracht, the Anne Frank Huis (Anne Frank House).

A secret refuge

The house at no. 263 was made famous by the diary kept by Anne Frank (1929–1945), whose Jewish family hid from the Nazis here in a tiny secret apartment behind her father's herb and spice warehouse. She started keeping the diary shortly after her 13th birthday, on 12 June 1942. The Franks went into hiding three weeks later, and – together with the Van Daan family and a dentist named Dussel – escaped discovery until August 1944, when they were betrayed to the Germans. Anne's father was the only one to survive the German concentration camps. The diary was found by an office cleaner and was published in 1947. It has been a bestseller ever since, and was filmed in 1959. The crowds of visitors make the visit to the tiny, empty apartment less than moving, but the permanent exhibition which occupies the rest of the building effectively evokes the horror of the Nazi Occupation and genocide.

Walk on down Prinsengracht towards the Westerkerk, designed by Hendrik de Keyser in 1619 and completed in 1638, after his death, by his son Pieter (1595–1676) and Cornelis Dancker, who added the florid globe and crown symbol granted to the city 150 years earlier by the Emperor Maximilian. The graceful Neoclassical interior, designed by Jacob van Campen, is lighter and airier than that of the nearby Noorderkerk; it has the shape of a double cross. The magnificent organ was decorated by Gerard de Lairesse (1641–1711), a pupil of Rembrandt's. Rembrandt himself is said to be buried here, although there is no sign of his tomb. A plaque marks the grave of Rembrandt's son Titus.

The Westertoren, the globe-crowned church tower, is Amsterdam's tallest at 85m (251ft). Climb to the top for a bird's-eye view of the city-centre, its rings of canals and, beneath you, the Jordaan district.

There is a better view of the Westerkerk from the other side of Prinsengracht, and crossing the canal also gives you an excuse to visit another venerable café with a claim to the title of Amsterdam's oldest. Turn right at the end of the bridge and you will find Café Chris at the corner of Prinsengracht and Bloemstraat. There has been a tavern here since 1624, and the builders working on the Westerkerk are said to have received their pay here. No doubt they drank part of it here as well.

Follow Prinsengracht round in a long curve southeastwards until you reach Spiegelgracht. Turn right here, towards the treasures of Museumplein. The short Spiegelgracht began to attract Amsterdam's smarter art and antiques dealers around the turn of the century, with the opening of the Rijksmuseum, the grand façade of which can be seen from its southern end. Almost 100 antiques dealers manage to squeeze into its 300m (1000ft) length, selling everything from almost affordable curios and collectibles to the rarest and costliest of fine furniture, archaeological finds, paintings and sculpture. At Spiegelgracht's southern end, cross first Lijnbaansgracht, then Weteringschans and Singelgracht to arrive on Stadhouderskade. Keep going past the Rijksmuseum to Museumplein and the Van Gogh Museum.

Van Gogh

The finest museum that we will visit on this walk (for the Rijksmuseum itself see page 60), and one of the most exciting in Amsterdam, is midway along the northwest side of Museumplein. The Rijksmuseum Vincent van Gogh (National Vincent van Gogh Museum) has the world's biggest and most varied collection of the man's work – 200 paintings and 500 drawings – and his own collection of engravings and Japanese prints, plus his letters to his brother Théo; there is also a fine assemblage of work by contemporaries, such as Paul Gauguin (1848–1903), Claude Monet (1840–1926) and Henri de Toulouse-Lautrec (1864–1901). The museum, a spacious, bright building, was completed in 1973.

Start on the ground floor, where a rotating exhibition provides an introduction to the painter's life, work and background. Vincent van Gogh (1854–1890) painted for less than ten years. In 1885, then 32 years old, he studied briefly at the Antwerp Academy; though he was influenced by some of his contemporaries, and by Japanese woodcut artists like Ando Hiroshige (1797–1858) – whose work had hardly been discovered in Europe – he was almost entirely self-taught. Looking at the glowing works here, it is hard to believe that his genius was barely recognized by his contemporaries. He sold only one painting in his lifetime, and lived almost entirely on advances from his younger brother Théo, an art dealer, who managed to make a far better living selling paintings than Vincent did painting them. Théo, too, died young, at the age of 32, and it was his widow Johanna who finally brought Vincent's work to a wider audience. Not long after Vincent's death, his paintings began to fetch high prices from galleries and collectors worldwide.

Go next to the first floor, where the permanent core collection of van Gogh's work hangs; the collection is rotated, changing constantly. In the two years before his death at the age of 37, van Gogh, then living in Arles, painted more than 200 works, ranging in subject matter from the muddy fields and leaden clouds of his native Netherlands to the brilliant colours and bright sunlight of Provence. At one end of the scale is the earthy Potato Eaters, redolent of northern European farm life; at the other is the almost hallucinogenic radiance of the various treatments of the sunflowers of southern France. The paintings from this final period of his life are grouped by theme, illustrating powerfully how van Gogh's treatment of the same subject might change almost from day to day as he discovered, invented and sharpened new techniques.

From the permanent collection, go on to the Print Room, still on the first floor, which gives some clues to van Gogh's earlier influences, notably the Japanese printmakers Kesai and Hiroshige.

Special exhibitions, usually of artists who had some connection with van Gogh, are held on the second and third floors of the museum.

The cutting edge of art

Leaving the Van Gogh Museum, turn left down Paulus Potterstraat (at the northwest side of Museumplein) to the Stedelijk Museum, whose bourgeois 19th-century exterior belies its adventurous contents. The Stedelijk is regarded as one of the world's leading museums of modern art and its permanent collection includes works by Monet, Paul Cézanne (1839–1906) and Pablo Picasso (1881–1973). Temporary exhibitions range from the weird but wonderful to the ridiculous – the museum sometimes seems to be trying too hard to stay at the cutting edge of the avant-garde – but are consistently interesting.

On entering the museum, climb the imposing marble staircase to the first floor, where there is a rotating exhibition of works from the permanent collection; among them should be some of the museum's lovely Cézanne landscapes, at least one of the handful of van Goghs left behind when the van Gogh collection moved to its own museum up the road, and works by Henri Matisse (1869–1964), Marc Chagall (1889–1985) and Wassily Kandinsky (1866–1944). The pop artists of the 1960s, including Andy Warhol (1926–1987) and Roy Lichtenstein (1923–), are well represented, and the museum's fine collection of work by living artists is an eye-opener.

Top billing goes to the unique collection of works by the Russian abstract painter Kazimir Malevich (1878–1935) and by the Dutch painters of the De Stijl movement, Piet Mondrian (1872–1944) and Theo van Doesberg (1883–1931). Malevich and his Dutch contemporaries worked separately through the years of World War I and the Russian Revolution, after which Malevich was unable to leave the Soviet Union. But their work is very much along the same lines in its drive to reduce art to the purely abstract by means of solid geometric shapes.

Walk downstairs to the Print Room, whose startlingly eclectic, ever-changing collection includes the work of contemporary photographers as well as poster- and print-makers from earlier decades.

Finally, visit the ground floor. As hinted, it sometimes seems the Stedelijk has inherited the provocative spirit of the 1960s and goes out of its way to provoke in the name of art. This is where the most innovative temporary exhibitions are held, many of them calculated to send you on your way pondering the nature of art.

Music and greenery

Exit the museum, turn left and, at the end of Paulus Potterstraat, left again on Van Baerlestraat; cross the street and walk to the grandiose pillared portico of the Concertgebouw (Concert Hall), a cultural landmark built in the 1880s by six Amsterdam entrepreneurs in a bid to erase the city's philistine reputation; among those who commented on the money-minded Amsterdammers' lack of culture was Johannes Brahms (1833–1897), who, invited to visit the city in 1879, characterized the Dutch as 'schlechte Musikanten' ('dreadful musicians') and bemoaned the lack of an acceptable venue for his music. Stung into action, the consortium hired the architect A.L. van Gendt (1835–1901) and saw the Dutch neo-Renaissance building completed in 1888. Its acoustics – as much by good luck as by good planning – are superb, and it has become a sought-after venue for orchestras and musicians from all over the world.

Cross Museumstraat and continue along Van Baerlestraat; this avenue becomes, after a slight leftward kink, Roelof Hartstraat, then crosses the Boerenwetering to become Ceintuur Baan; at the end of this street, turn left into the Sarphatipark. This small patch of green is named after Samuel Sarphati (1813–1866), the energetic doctor and do-gooder who almost single-handedly dragged Amsterdam out of the torpor and squalor which beset it in the early 19th century. Sarphati seems to have been one of those individuals with the ability to be everywhere at the same time, doing several things at once; among his innovations were a garbage-removal service (it made a profit selling the city's trash to farmers as pig-food and fertilizer), a building company, a bank, an industrial-development organization and an exhibition centre. The pretty little park hardly seems a big enough memorial.

Keeping the park on your right, walk up its side and keep going along Eerste (1e) Van der Helststraat. Now take the second street on your right, Albert Cuypstraat.

A market to savour

This is the venue of Amsterdam's sprawling Albert Cuypstraat Market, which spills over into the surrounding streets for more than 1km (half a mile). This is a far cry from the tatty bohemianism of the Waterlooplein Fleamarket; it is a noisy, bustling expanse of stalls and shops where, if you are prepared to look hard enough, you can buy just about anything. Shopping is a hungry business, and there are plenty of stalls whose reason for being there is to fortify peckish shoppers for further rummaging through the piles of fresh fruit and vegetables, herbs, spices, tea, coffee . . . you name it; there are also plenty of ethnic restaurants (mainly Indonesian and Surinamese). It is a good place to stock up on excellent Dutch coffee, cheeses, chocolates and other Amsterdam delicacies to take home.

Walk along Albert Cuypstraat to its northeastern end, turn left along Van Wou Straat to cross Singelgracht, continue along what is now Westeinde and then right to cross the Amstel River by the Sarphatistraat Bridge, named, like the park, after the philanthropic doctor. Turning left again, walk up the river to the imposing, domed front of the Theatre Carré, built in 1887 by the impresario Oscar Carré to house his permanent circus. The circus did not outlive its founder and, since the beginning of the 20th century, the building has been a venue for opera and operetta. Turn right along Nieuwe Prinsengracht, then walk down Weesperstraat to Weesperplein Metro station, the conclusion of this walk.

Markets and the Amstel

This walk features pauses at several lively markets and a view of the River Amstel, the source of so much of Amsterdam's early prosperity, plus a visit to the Amsterdam Historical Museum. In colder weather, you might want to cut this walk short at the Blauw Brug, missing the stretch along the outer Amstel. When the weather is fine you can make a day of it by linking up with the Plantage and Artis Zoo walk (see page 65).

Start: Dam; trams 4, 9, 14, 16, 24, 25

Finish: Waterlooplein; Metro, trams 4, 9

Length: 4.8km (3 miles)

Time: 4hr

Refreshments: Clusters of pleasant taverns and cafés around the Spui and the Rembrandtplein, and lots of others along the way; restaurants in the Amsterdams Historisch Museum and the Stopera

Which day: This walk takes in two to three markets on any day, so which day you choose may depend on your special interests. The Flower Market, one of Amsterdam's most popular attractions, is open every day except Sunday, and the Waterlooplein Fleamarket is open daily. See below for other opening times.

To visit:
- Nieuwezijds Voorburgwal Postzegelmarkt (stamp market): Wednesday and Saturday 13.00–16.00
- Amsterdams Historisch Museum (Amsterdam Historical Museum): Monday–Friday 10.00–17.00, Saturday–Sunday 11.00–17.00
- Spui Boekenmarkt (book market): Friday 10.00–18.00
- Spui Kunstmarkt (art market): Sunday 10.00–18.00
- Bloemenmarkt (flower market): Monday–Saturday 09.30–17.00
- Thorbeckeplein Kunstmarkt (art market): March–October Sunday 10.30–18.00
- Willet–Holthuysen Museum: Monday–Friday 10.00–17.00, Saturday–Sunday 11.00–17.00
- Waterlooplein Fleamarket: Monday–Friday 09.00–17.00, Saturday 08.30–17.30
- Het Rembrandthuis: Monday–Saturday 10.00–17.00, Sunday 13.00–17.00
- Joods Historisch Museum (Jewish Historical Museum): daily 11.00–17.00

Leaving the Dam, turn right onto Paleisstraat, walk past the south wall of the Royal Palace, and turn left onto Nieuwezijds Voorburgwal for the Postzegelmarkt (stamp

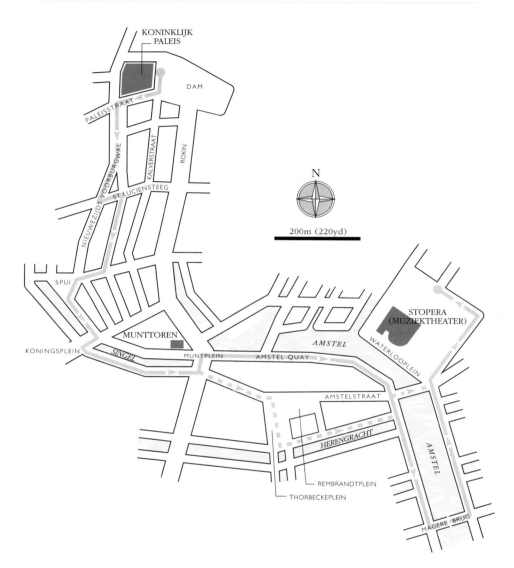

market). This takes place twice a week by the corner of Wijde Steeg and Nieuwezijds Voorburgwal, where a dozen or so stalls display not only vast albums of colourful and historic stamps but clinking heaps of coins, military medals and cap badges.

Cross the street to the east side of Nieuwezijds Voorburgwal and, about 150m (165yd) south of the stamp market, turn left into Sint Luciensteeg. Set into the wall of the Amsterdams Historisch Museum, on the right-hand side of this narrow passage, are numerous traditional gablestones, salvaged from demolished homes. The largest depicts a goldsmith at work; others show domestic beasts, tradesmen and their tools.

The story of the city

The Amsterdams Historisch Museum is housed in one of the city's oldest buildings, the 15th-century Convent of St Lucy, which was taken over by the city in 1578 and became the Burgerweeshuis (municipal orphanage). In 1975 the old orphanage was converted into a museum, which now offers a vivid combination of modern exhibitions and older memorabilia, spanning the centuries, all intelligently laid out in twenty exhibition rooms. The museum does far more than simply display remnants of Amsterdam's history; instead, it leads you through that history – revealing, for example, how Golden Age Amsterdam had only just above 200,000 residents, less than a quarter of the city's present-day population . . . something that makes Amsterdam's achievements seem even more astounding.

All twenty rooms merit careful inspection but, if time is limited, you should certainly not miss the museum's high-points. First, climb the giddy spiral stair to the Bell Room, where the 17th-century bells from the Munttoren (see page 51) are on display and where you can hear recorded chimes from the Royal Palace and the city's three great churches. Room 5 shows the paths taken by Amsterdam's merchant adventurers, a graphic reminder of the extent of the city's 16th- and 17th-century trading empire – which, by the turn of the 17th century, spanned the entire known world and was at the cutting edge throughout the era of exploration.

Even if you do not intend to pause here for refreshment, look into the museum's ground floor restaurant, In de Oude Goliath, for a glimpse of Goliath himself, in the shape of a gigantic armoured statue whose helmet-plumes touch the roof beams. Next to him stands a tiny, life-sized David.

The final must is the Schuttergalerij (guards' gallery), by which you leave the museum. This unique gallery is lined with group portraits of the militia companies first formed in the late 14th century to police and defend the city. Amsterdam's leading painters – among them Rembrandt and Frans Hals (*c.*1580–1666) – portrayed the watch companies of their day (see pages 62 and 119); although the portraits here are by less famous artists, they are no less revealing, especially those depicting company banquets, some of which beg for cartoon-style speech bubbles.

The Schuttergalerij leads onto Gedempte Begijnsloot, a narrow lane of white-washed houses which brings you, via a stone archway on your right, to a tranquil, tree-filled square: the Begijnhof.

Good sisters

This open green space can offer a welcome respite from the people-packed streets of the city-centre. Walk first to no. 34, the oldest house in Amsterdam, dating from the 15th century. It is impossible to miss – it is the last surviving wooden house in the city. As Amsterdam's population exploded (from 10,000 in 1475 to 100,000 a century later), houses were packed closer and closer together and wooden buildings became an ever-greater fire risk. After several devastating conflagrations, the municipality banned all-wood buildings in 1521. Above the door, no. 34 bears the legend Het Wouten Huys: The Wooden House. Immediately in front of it is a monument to the Beguines or Begijns, the 14th-century order of lay sisters who founded their community here in 1346. They rejected the cloistered life of the nunnery – each sister had her own small house and was not subject to the rule of a Mother Superior – but devoted their lives to helping the ill and the poor. In the centre of the square is the original Begijnkerk Chapel, built in 1419. The Begijns were deprived of their church, but not their other properties, in 1578, during the Reformation; it stood empty until 1607, when it was taken over by Presbyterian refugees from England, and is still known as the English Church. Despite its changes of use, it still retains the only unaltered medieval church tower in the city. Meanwhile, like other Catholics in the post-Reformation Netherlands, the Begijns had to worship clandestinely: their 'secret' church, next to Het Wouten Huys, is still in use. The last of the Begijns, Sister Antonia, died in 1971; the pretty little apartments around the square now house elderly widows.

Books and paintings

From the south side of the Begijnhof, an arched alleyway leads to the Spui, which is among Amsterdam's most pleasant public spaces. In the middle of the square is one of the city's favourite symbols, the bronze statue of a grinning urchin, cap tipped to the back of his head, arms akimbo and socks drooping around his ankles. This is Het Lieverdje (Little Darling), the embodiment of a tradition of irreverent resistance to authority that Amsterdam has maintained since the time of Philip II of Spain and his ambitions of conquest.

If you arrive at the Spui on a Friday you'll find the square crammed with stalls selling antiquarian books and prints (the Boekenmarkt). On a Sunday it is taken over by the art market (the Kunstmarkt), with booths selling everything from pretty ceramics to surrealist oils. The quality of the work varies wildly: some of it is exciting and adventurous, some competent but uninspired, and some totally lacking any discernible merit.

Leaving the Spui from its southwest corner, you find yourself facing the Singel, the earliest and innermost of the canals which ring the city-centre. Singel means 'moat', and in the 15th century this was not only a waterway and drainage channel but an integral part of the city's defences. Turn left and follow the canal, then turn right to cross the bridge into Koningsplein and the Bloemenmarkt (flower market). This floating market is one of Amsterdam's most-hyped tourism attractions yet, looking at the row of functional pontoon-booths from the bridge, you may wonder what all the fuss is about. The enclosed booths open onto the street, so it is not until you reach the Bloemenmarkt Quay that you see their floral glories. But, even so, though the displays are pretty enough, this single row of flower- and plant-sellers is not all it is generally cracked up to be and, unless you are a fanatical gardener, the market is hardly worth a special trip. On a sunny spring day, though, the stalls – overflowing with potted plants and cut flowers – make a typical Amsterdam shot for your camera.

Walk on along the south quay of the Singel. Your next landmark is plainly visible. The Munttoren (Mint Tower) is another Hendrik de Keyser confection: if you have already seen some of his other towers and spires around the city, such as that of the Zuiderkerk (see page 30), you will recognize his style. The Munttoren, built in 1622, stands on the site of the earlier Regulierspoort, the south gate into the city, overlooking the Singel and the wider waters of the Binnen (Inner) Amstel. The mint of the Dutch Republic was relocated to Amsterdam from Utrecht in 1672, when much of the Netherlands was occupied by the French armies of Louis XIV.

Louis originally invaded the Spanish territories to the south, inducing the Dutch to ally with England and Sweden in order to check French expansion. In 1670 England switched sides: Charles II of England and Scotland detested the Dutch for their Protestantism, while Louis XIV of France hated them for their republicanism: the Dutch were attacked by land and sea. In the six-year war that followed they stood off French armies and English sea-power, but a revolution toppled the republic from within. This brought to power a young prince of the House of Orange who – through marriage to a Stuart princess – was eventually to become William III of England and Scotland, and Europe's bitterest opponent of French power.

Hand-painted porcelain

If Delft porcelain is your thing, you will want to pause here, because the Munttoren houses the biggest and best of Amsterdam's china shops: De Porcelyne Fles (The China Bottle) claims to offer every design ever produced at the Delft factory. It is a branch of the Delft company of the same name, the last surviving maker of authentic hand-painted Delftware.

If you are here on a Sunday, leave Muntplein by the Reguliersbreestraat for a look at the Thorbeckeplein Kunstmarkt (art market). As with its counterpart in the Spui, the standard of the works displayed here is a matter of pot luck, but there is always something different to look at. Leaving the market, turn left along Herengracht and walk towards the Blauw Brug (Blue Bridge). The Willet–Holthuysen Museum at no. 605 Herengracht is a beautifully preserved example of a gracious canal-side home (see page 38 for details).

Alternatively, walk across the Muntplein to leave it via the Amstel Quay, which runs along the south side of the Amstel Basin. Opposite are the modern buildings of the Stopera complex, which houses the National Ballet, the Netherlands Dance Theatre, the Netherlands Opera and the new Stadhuis (Town Hall). Controversy surrounded the building of the complex in the 1980s: the older buildings torn down to make way for it had long been occupied by Amsterdam's highly effective squatter movement, and there were bitter clashes with police as they were evicted.

Keep along the Amstel Quay until you reach the Blauw Brug (Blue Bridge). This is nowadays not blue at all. This imposing 19th-century stone and cast-iron bridge replaced an earlier one which had traditionally been painted in the blue of the Dutch national flag. Built in 1883, the modern Blauw Brug is a copy of Paris's Pont Alexandre. Each of its stone piers is shaped like the prow of a boat, and decorative totem-pole-like columns are adorned with Classical capitals and yellow crowns. It is perhaps the only one of Amsterdam's many bridges which can be described as elegant, and yet it aroused controversy when it was built — because some dourer citizens felt its elegance was a scandalous waste of tax-payers' money!

On a cold winter's day, you may want to walk briskly across the Blauw Brug to reach the Waterlooplein Fleamarket directly. On a sunny day, though, do not cross the bridge but carry on for a stroll beside the Amstel, envying the river-dwellers whose houseboats are moored along the banks (on a chilly day in March, by contrast, life on the water seems less enviable). Walk down as far as the 80m (250ft) Magere Brug. A bridge has spanned the canal here since the 17th century, when, according to legend, a footbridge was built for two sisters who lived on this side of the Amstel and wanted easy access to their carriage and horses, stabled on the other shore. Their family name, so the tale goes, was Magere; but magere means 'skinny', and so it may just as likely have been called the 'Skinny Bridge' because of its narrow girth. It was widened in 1772, becoming a double drawbridge. The present structure is a copy, built in 1929.

Cross the Magere Brug — you may have to wait for a string of barges to pass through the swinging section — and turn left, heading back up the opposite bank of the Amstel towards the final market on this walk, the Waterlooplein Fleamarket. Turn right onto Waterlooplein at the east end of the Blauw Brug. The market is held on the open space behind the Stopera, running between Waterlooplein and the Zwanenburgwal Canal. The market is a clutter of stalls selling neo-hippie gear, cheap jewellery, junk, old clothes and perhaps even the occasional genuine antique. Overlooking it is the portico of the Mozes en Aaronkerk (Moses and Aaron Church), built in 1841 on the site of one of Amsterdam's 'secret' Catholic churches.

Before ending this walk, you may want to visit two of Amsterdam's major attractions, each within 50m (55yd) of Waterlooplein. These are the Rembrandthuis (Rembrandt's home — see page 32), at 4–6 Jodenbreestraat, and the Jewish Historical Museum (see page 33), at 2–4 Jonas Daniel Meijerplein.

To combine this walk with the Plantage and Artis Zoo walk, starting at Waterlooplein, turn to page 65.

The Jordaan

This zigzag walk passes through Amsterdam's prettiest district, bordered by the Prinsengracht, Brouwersgracht, Lijnbaansgracht and Looiersgracht canals. The Jordaan's higgledy-piggledy houses once lined a watery maze of small canals, most of them − like Lindengracht and Anjeliersgracht − now filled in. These had been expanded from the original ditches dug to drain the area that would contain housing for Amsterdam's fast-expanding population. Before that, this was a district of slums and factories outside the ring of new canals − Herengracht, Keizersgracht and Prinsengracht. It became the favoured resort of the rich and fashionable at the beginning of the 17th century. The area's name is said to derive from the French jardin (garden), a legacy of the Protestant Huguenot refugees who escaped Catholic France to settle here in the 17th century, just when the Jordaan was being built and planted with trees. Its tree-girt streets and canals are at their prettiest in early summer.

Start:	Stationsplein; Metro, all trams and buses
Finish:	Leidseplein; trams 1, 2, 5, 6, 7, 10, 11
Length:	6.4km (4 miles)
Time:	3hr
Refreshments:	Plenty of 'brown cafés' and other cafés all along the walk, with a concentration of places to eat and drink at Leidseplein (though many of these are very touristy)
Which day:	Not Friday or Sunday
To visit:	● Boerenmarkt (Noordermarkt): Saturday 09.00–17.00 (produce and caged birds), Monday 09.00–17.00 (bric-à-brac)
	● Antiquemarkt de Looier (Looier Antique Market): Saturday–Wednesday 11.00–17.00; Thursday 11.00–21.00
	● Rommelmarkt (fleamarket): Saturday–Thursday 11.00–17.00

The Jordaan remained for centuries a tough working-class neighbourhood with a tradition of sullen resistance to authority. Angry workers rioted here during the 1930s, and it wasn't until Amsterdam began the long task of repairing the damage of World War II that the government began to clean up the district and provide decent housing and services. By the 1960s the Jordaan had become the trendy place to be, but its traditional rebelliousness prevented it being completely taken over by upwardly mobile professionals seeking quaint homes to refurbish. There were strong protests against gentrification.

The response was the creation of a stock of affordable state housing which ensured the Jordaan has retained some of its down-to-earth character, so that you can find here − alongside its scattering of bohemian hangouts and coffee-shops dating from the 1960s, its trendy restaurants, nightspots and art galleries − the finest concentration of

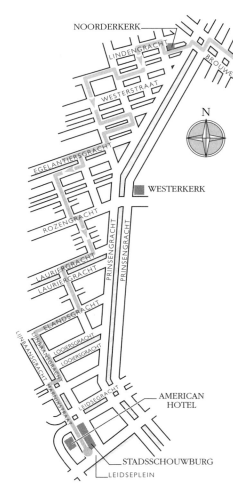

NOORDERKERK

LINDENGRACHT

BROUWERSGRACHT

PRINS

CENTRAAL STATION

HENDRIKKADE

WESTERSTRAAT

N

SINGEL

400m (440yd)

EGELANTIERSGRACHT

WESTERKERK

ROZENGRACHT

PRINSENGRACHT

PRINSENGRACHT

LAURIERGRACHT

LAURIERGRACHT

ELANDSGRACHT

LOOIERSGRACHT

LIJNBAANSGRACHT

LINDBAANSGRACHT

LOOIERSGRACHT

MARNIXSTRAAT

LEIDSEGRACHT

AMERICAN HOTEL

STADSSCHOUWBURG

LEIDSEPLEIN

Amsterdam's murky, smoke-darkened 'brown cafés'. To see the Jordaan at its bohemian best, try to be here for its ten-day autumn festival in September, when drinking, dining, dancing, contests and processions spill into the streets (and sometimes into the canals, too).

Even more than the rest of inner Amsterdam, the Jordaan is a place where it pays to look up as you walk. Decorative gables, in a variety of styles, and fine gablestones – frequently witty modern ones inspired by the older tradition – adorn many buildings.

Leaving Stationsplein, cross the Open Haven to Prins Hendrikkade and turn right. Cross the Singel, turning left at the end of the bridge, then right to walk along the north bank of Brouwersgracht.

The small square at the junction of Brouwersgracht and Herengracht is the Herenmarkt, and the building backing onto it is the Westindische Huis (West India House), once the headquarters of the Dutch West India Company. A statue of Peter Stuyvesant (1592–1672), first governor of Nieuw Amsterdam – the Dutch settlement on Manhattan Island which was to become New York – stands in the courtyard, the only part of the building that is now open to the public.

The Brewers' Canal

Brouwersgracht – 'Brewers' Canal' – was once the heart of the city's brewing trade, with hundreds of small breweries supplying homes as well as alehouses. In

Amsterdam's early days, beer was a far healthier drink than water and cheaper than tea or coffee, which were both novel and very expensive. By 1500, Amsterdam's canals were so filthy that drinking water had to be brought into the city by barge from the relatively clean River Vecht, then distributed via smaller vessels. In winter the rivers might freeze, making drinking water even more expensive and scarce. Not surprisingly, beer was a popular alternative. Twin dolphins support the neck-gable at no. 48.

Follow Brouwersgracht until you reach the Papiermolensluis Bridge, where the canal meets Prinsengracht. Turn left across this, then sharp right across Prinsengracht on the Lekkeresluis Bridge to enter the Jordaan proper. Follow the canal down to the Noordermarkt's square, dominated by the Noorderkerk (see page 42 for further details of this church). Turn right along the top of the square, looking out for the cow on the gablestone of no. 17, the chicken on no. 18 and the sheep on no. 19, all dating from the 16th and 17th centuries, when the square was a livestock market. Turn right to leave the square by Noorderkerkstraat, then left onto Lindengracht, where at no. 55 you should be able to spot one of the Jordaan's more obscure gablestones. The motto reads 'Hcardenil' and the crest depicts fish nesting in the branches of a tree – symbolic of 'the world turned upside down', a popular sentiment among medieval radical reformers. It takes a little time to puzzle out what 'Hcardenil' means: it is 'Lindengracht' (more or less) spelt back-to-front and upside-down.

A slippery pastime

Lindengracht was the scene of one of the Jordaan's many riots when, on 25 July 1886, an officious policeman tried to halt a traditional eel-pulling contest (a sort of tug-o'-war using a live eel smeared with soap to make it even more slippery). The crowd objected, the policeman was bundled into a cellar, and police reinforcements were showered with flowerpots and roof-tiles. Eventually the army was called in to restore order. In the three-day riot, 26 people were killed and hundreds injured.

Turn left off Lindengracht onto Eerste Lindendwarsstraat, crossing Lindenstraat, and walk down to Boomstraat, where you turn right. No. 61 has another typical gablestone, a crowned star, and the date 1663. Turn right into Tweede Boomdwarsstraat and immediately left into Karthuizersstraat, named after the 15th-century Carthusian abbey, of which no trace remains. At no. 89, however, a doorway leads into the Karthuizershofje, also called the Huys–Zitten–Wedeuwen–Hofje (Widows' House), one of the largest of the city's almshouses. Amsterdam was among the first cities to develop a municipal social conscience, and from the 17th century provided these hofjes as subsidized housing for the elderly and needy. The Karthuizershofje was built in 1650 to provide homes for needy widows, and it still offers subsidized housing for young people. The architect was Daniel Stalpaert (1615–1676). Look out for the two sea-monster-shaped handpumps in the courtyard and for the arms of the city – a sailing ship and three St Andrew's crosses – on the inner walls.

At the end of Karthuizersstraat turn left onto Tichelstraat. Many of the Jordaan's streets are named for flowers or trees; Lindengracht, for example, means Lime Canal. Others are named for the tradesmen who worked there. Tichelstraat (Tile Street) was the home and workplace of the district's many tilemakers.

At the end of the street, cross Westerstraat, known as Anjeliersgracht (Carnation Canal) until 1861, when it was filled in to provide wider access for carts. For most of the week, this is an uninteresting traffic artery, but if you take this walk on a Monday morning you will find it jam-packed with the white canvas awnings of market stalls selling everything from pickled herrings and fresh fruit to nuts, bolts, tools and electrical bits and pieces.

Walk down Tweede Anjelierdwarsstraat, the Jordaan's trendiest shopping, eating and drinking street.

Method or madness
You will have noticed a number of the district's side-streets bear the prefix 1e (eerste, first) or 2e (tweede, second), or even 3e (derde, third), combined with the suffix dwarsstraat (cross-street). The system is easy enough once you get the hang of it. Cross-streets are numbered from east to west and named after the main street they connect with. Tweede (2e) Egelantiersdwarsstraat, for example, is the second cross-street off Egelantiersgracht. Tweede Anjelierdwarsstraat is the joker in the pack – it is the second cross-street off Westerstraat, which was formerly Anjeliersgracht, as noted above. Like other cross-streets, it changes its name block by block, becoming – in less than 300m (330yd) – successively Tweede Tuindwarsstraat, then Tweede Egelantiersdwarsstraat.

Tweede Tuinddwarsstraat is the busiest section of this thoroughfare at the heart of the Jordaan. At its end, turn left into Tuinstraat, an uneasy mix of modern buildings and older houses. Cross it and turn right onto Eerste Egelantiersdwarsstraat. There are two tradesmen's gablestones worth looking out for here. On no. 19 two bakers stand by their glowing oven, while next door at no. 21 an arm brandishing a hammer indicates the home and workshop of a goldsmith. On the corner of Eerste Egelantiersdwarsstraat and Tuinstraat is a modern gablestone depicting Jan Pieterszoon Sweelinck (1562–1621), the 16th-century organist. This building is the Claes Claeszoon Hofje, the entrance to which is just around the corner in Eerste Egelantiersdwarsstraat. Surrounding three quiet courtyards, it is the home of the Sweelinck Music School.

From its doorway carry on along Eerste Egelantiersdwarsstraat onto Egelantiersstraat, and turn right, then left into Tweede Egelantiersdwarsstraat, which quickly leads you to one of the Jordaan's prettiest canals and one of its finest old cafés. Café 't Smalle, at no. 12 Egelantiersgracht, was opened in 1786 by Pieter Hoppe, one of the city's most famous distillers, as a distillery and proeflokaal (tasting-house), where potential customers could try the product before buying in quantity. In those days

Plate 9: *The Magere Brug on the Amstel River is prettily lit up at night (see the Markets and the Amstel walk, page 52).*

Plate 10: *Looking west over the Jordaan district from the Westerkerk tower. A real Jordaaner is born within earshot of the Westerkerk chimes (see the Jordaan walk, page 53).*

Plate 11: *The Rijksmuseum is not only a treasury of painting and sculpture but one of the city's most splendid buildings (see the Rijksmuseum and the Vondelpark walk, page 60).*

Plate 12: *Artwork of all types and periods adorns both the inside and outside of the Rijksmuseum (see the Rijksmuseum and the Vondelpark walk, page 60).*

Plate 13: The palatial interior of the Nationaal Vakbondsmuseum (National Trades Union Museum), designed by H.P. Berlage, who called it his most successful work (see the Plantage and the Artis Zoo walk, page 67).

Plate 14: The entrance to the Hortus Botanicus or Botanical Gardens, one of urban Amsterdam's treasured stretches of greenery (see the Plantage and the Artis Zoo walk, page 66).

Plate 15: *The high point of a walk around the Oosterdok (East Harbour) is a view of the replica East Indiaman, the* Amsterdam *(see the Oosterdok: The East Harbour walk, page 73).*

Plate 16: *For long a self-contained community, the Western Islands are now becoming a desirable address for the upwardly-mobile (see the Westelijk Eilanden: The Western Islands walk, page 75).*

quality-control was less thorough than it is now, and each batch of geniever might be different from the last, so customers expected a free sample. Today you have to pay for your tasting sessions in the city's surviving proeflokaalen! This is one of the finest, restored to its pristine state in the 1970s.

Geniever, Amsterdam's traditional spirit, is similar to gin but much more strongly flavoured. It gets its name from ginebra, the Spanish word for juniper, which is its main flavouring, but other herbs such as caraway and coriander can also go into the mix. Locals use lots of slang terms for a shot of geniever and the beer chaser that often goes with it. Ask for a borrel, a hassebassie, a keiltje, a neutje, a pikketanussie, a recht op en neer or a slokkie – the barman will know what you mean. None of these terms is readily translatable, but some others are: to show off, ask for a kamelenrug (camel's back) or an over het Ij kijkertje (look over the Ij) – a glass so brim full it cannot be lifted without spilling it. The approved way of dealing with this is to leave the glass on the counter and bring your lips to it. A beer chaser is a kopstoot (knock on the head), a kabouter pils (dwarf pils) or lampie licht (little lamp), and a large glass of ale a bakkie (jar) or a vaas (vase). Whatever beer you order, expect about half the glassful to be froth.

Canals, jumble and hippiedom

Cross the bridge at the corner of Derde (3e) Egelantiersstraat and turn left along the south side of the canal. If the doorway between no. 107 and no. 114 is open, look into the St Andrieshofje, where access to a peaceful courtyard is gained by an alley lined with blue-and-white tiles from Delft.

Turn left into Derde Leliedwarsstraat and follow this cross-street to Bloemgracht. This used to be the home of the Jordaan's élite, the master craftsmen of various trades, and was ironically known as the district's answer to Herengracht, where Amsterdam's wealthiest families lived. Turning left, look across the canal for three of its more striking houses, all next door to each other at nos. 87–91, each indicated by its gablestone: they are the Steeman (townsman), Landman (farmer) and Seeman (sailor), each of these 17th-century homes being adorned with a portrait in stone of its occupant, in appropriate dress. Follow the north (even-numbered) side of Bloemgracht to no. 38, where André Coppenhagen's shop is an irresistible Aladdin's cave of beads and baubles. There are hundreds of different shapes, sizes and colours on display in huge glass jars.

From here, double back to the bridge and cross Bloemgracht, then walk onwards to Rozengracht. This part of the Jordaan is less entertaining: most of its canals have been filled in, and Rozengracht itself is a rather nondescript traffic artery. Cross it, go slightly left, then right along Eerste Rozendwarsstraat and Eerste Laurierdwarsstraat to Lauriergracht. Turn right and left over the first bridge you reach and walk down Hazenstraat to Elandsgracht, where you find the first of the Jordaan's two antique and junk markets. Both are indoors, making them ideal browsing-places on a wet day.

Enter the Looier market at no. 109 Elandsgracht to become immediately completely disoriented. It seems the only way to be sure of retracing your steps out of this labyrinth of stalls, piled high with the clutter of centuries, is − like Theseus − to carry a ball of string and pay it out as you go. The Looier market is always changing. Some stalls are more or less permanent fixtures, specializing in a favourite genre − antique brassware, say, or glass bottles, or jewellery. Others seem to stock anything they can lay their hands on as long as it is old. Among the clutter, though, those with an eye for such things may find real antiques. Look out for relics of Amsterdam's long-lasting connection with the Far East.

Eventually emerging from the Looier market, turn left at the corner of Elandsgracht and Lijnbaansgracht and left again onto Looiersgracht, where at no. 38 you can plunge into an even more glorious permanent jumble-sale, the Looiersgracht Rommelmarkt. If you enjoy rummaging through the most unpromising piles to ferret out a collectible treasure, you will love the Rommelmarkt. At weekends, especially, it seems that this is where items end up when they have failed to find a buyer in any of the many other city markets. Jumble purists say this market is at its best on Saturday and Sunday, when you never know what you will find. Wednesday is also a jumble day; Monday is the day for coins and stamps, Tuesday is for books and records, and Thursday is for used and antique clothes. Whichever day you go, there is a certain camaraderie among the Rommelmarkt's stallholders and customers, as if they all understand that junk and jumble are far more interesting than any brand-new purchase could ever be.

From here, walk back to the corner of Looiersgracht and Lijnbaansgracht, turn left, then right to cross the Lijnbaansgracht; turn left again onto Marnixstraat, which leads you to Leidseplein and the end of this walk. The hulking, overblown Stadsschouwburg (City Theatre) at no. 26 Liedseplein is the square's biggest landmark; it was the home of the National Opera and Netherlands Ballet until they moved to the Stopera building (see page 32) on the Inner Amstel.

Just before you reach Leidseplein, stop at the bunker-like brick building at no. 334 Lijnbaansgracht. This is the Melkweg, a time-honoured survivor of the 1960s and early 1970s when Amsterdam established itself as the counter-culture capital of Europe. Then a disused cinema, it was the venue for countless happenings and free concerts. Moving with the times, it has grown into a cutting-edge venue for all sorts of experimental performance and high-tech art: arcane talk of new music and netsurfing mingles amiably with the mellow whiff of marijuana. On the other side of Leidseplein, the Paradiso − like the Melkweg a one-time cinema − is another hippie-era survivor, these days attracting big-name rock concerts.

The Leidseplein is the place to be on a summer's evening or a winter's afternoon. It and the smaller streets around it are packed with bars and cafés (more than 100 of them) offering every kind of live music, and in summer almost the entire square is a near-solid mass of café tables, providing the ever-changing cast of street performers with a captive audience. Whether or not you're tired at the end of your walk, what better to do than to rest here for a while, soaking up the ambience? After you've done that, if the day is still young, you might feel refreshed enough to carry straight on and do our next walk.

The Rijksmuseum and the Vondelpark

The Rijksmuseum is one of the finest museums of art in the world, with an immense collection of superb paintings and other works of art. You can easily spend all day here, and the impact of the collection is such that trying to combine a visit to the Rijksmuseum with a trip to the nearby Van Gogh Museum is to find yourself floundering in too much of a good thing; instead, take in Van Gogh's and other works on our Prinsengracht walk (see page 44). In summer, the Vondelpark is a welcome splash of green after the intensely man-made scenery of the historic city-centre. In wintry weather, you may want to omit the Vondelpark section of the walk in favour of spending more time in the warm museum.

Start/finish: Leidseplein; trams 1, 2, 5, 6, 7,10, 11, bus 63
Length: 3.2km (2 miles)
Time: All day
Refreshments: Cafes in the museums and in the Vondelpark
Which day: Not Monday
To visit:
- Rijksmuseum (National Museum): daily 10.00–17.00
- Vondelpark Openlucht Theater (Vondelpark Open-Air Theatre): summer festival performances June–August, Wednesday–Sunday, afternoon and evening
- Nederlands Filmmuseum: exhibitions daily 12.00–19.00; films daily 16.00–21.30

Leaving behind the bars and street entertainers of Leidseplein, cross Singelgracht by the bridge and turn left along Stadhouderskade, following the water to the grand brick pile of the Rijksmuseum, an unmistakable landmark occupying the corner of Museumstraat and Stadhouderskade. The red-brick Romanesque façade of the museum may remind you of Centraal Station: it was built by the same architect, P.J.H. Cuypers, and was a very controversial project in its day. Staid Amsterdammers thought it altogether too fancy, but before long it became the pride of the city.

A treasury of paintings

The nucleus of the museum's treasury of art is the collection of some 200 paintings amassed by Prince William V (1748–1806), who was driven into exile in 1798. It has been added to as patriotic art collectors and patrons of the arts have left their acquisitions to the nation. The new museum to house all this opened in 1885, and has expanded steadily ever since. It now contains more than 5000 paintings, a million prints and drawings, and tens of thousands of sculptures and other art objects. A complete guide to every work on display would be a book (or even books) in itself; this walk attempts to take in the highlights of the collection, including the works of

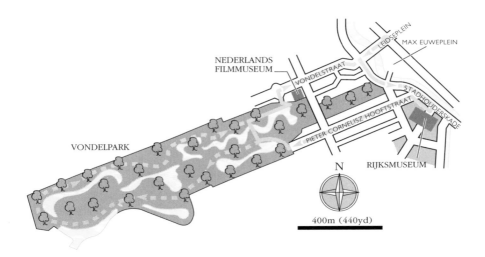

the most famous Dutch masters. The paintings are exhibited in rotation, so a specific work may not always hang in exactly the same place. A detailed guide to the museum's other rooms and displays is available from the information desk in the first-floor foyer.

Enter the Rijksmuseum from the north side, where two entrances (not always both in use) face onto the Stadhouderskade.

The jewels of the Rijksmuseum collection are on the first floor, where room after room of pictures trace the course of Dutch painting from the stiff religious art of the early medieval era to the increasingly easy and fluid styles of the Renaissance and the Golden Age, when painters broke free of the formalism and exclusively religious themes of earlier centuries.

From the central foyer and information desk on the north floor, turn left into a labyrinth of exhibition rooms. The paintings are in approximate chronological order, putting the works of masters like Frans Hals (c.1580–1666), Jacob van Ruisdael (c.1628-1682) and Jan Vermeer (1632-1675) into the context of their times, and there is a sense of mounting excitement as you approach the glories of the 17th-century masters. Each room, however, contains its own special treasures.

Rooms 201–204 are filled with medieval works, virtually all with religious themes, like the series of panels by the Master of Alkmaar (fl.1490–1510), *The Seven Works of Charity*, dating from 1504.

Carry on around the gallery, detouring into Room 207, a tiny circular annexe whose walls are covered with delightful miniature portraits and landscapes; two perfect landscapes by Jan Brueghel the Elder (1568–1625) – neither of them bigger than 15cm × 23cm (6in × 9in) – are among the larger pieces displayed here.

Enter Room 208 to meet one of the really big names: Frans Hals, whose works dominate this and the next two rooms. The most immediately recognizable image here is the lively portrait of the cheerfully dishevelled *Merry Drinker*.

A left turn into Room 211 brings you to the first of the Rijksmuseum's many Rembrandts. This room usually displays the painter's early work, and those of previous masters who influenced him, like his teacher Pieter Lastman (1593–1633). From here you pass through a series of rooms dominated by monumental landscapes and finely detailed representations from Classical and Biblical mythology; every picture tells a story – with a vengeance. Side-by-side with these are the works of contemporary realist painters. No less idealized, their work drew on actual rather than imagined landscapes – and was far less highly prized by buyers, who were slow to forsake their liking for the fantastical.

Rooms 215 and 216 are dominated by 17th-century portraits and family groups; the lively portraits by Jan Steen (1626–1679) of himself and his family are full of charm and mark a departure from the solemn portrayals of the city's wealthy and powerful.

Landscapes and townscapes adorn Rooms 217–221, and by now you may be hard put to contain your impatience, because the high-point of the Rijksmuseum's collection beckons. Before reaching it, though, detour right into Room 221A, which contains four perfect small works by Jan Vermeer: *The Milkmaid*, *The Little Street*, *Woman Reading a Letter* and *The Love Letter*. Their almost photographic realism alone makes them stand out from their neighbours, whose style always verges on the heavy-handed. Vermeer was not the most prolific of painters: the four works exhibited here represent ten per cent of his lifetime's output.

The Night Watch

Walk through Room 223 to reach Room 224 and Rembrandt's best-known work, *The Guard Company of Captain Frans Banning Cocq and Lieutenant Willem van Ruijtenburch*, better known as *The Night Watch*. Restoration – following vandalism in 1975 – has revealed how wide of the mark that nickname is: the company of arquebusiers are shown not on night patrol but in sunlight, which provides a bright contrast as they emerge from the shadows of a city gateway. Over the centuries since Rembrandt had completed it, the painting's colours darkened as a consequence of time and dirt, giving rise to the misleading alias. The huge painting (3.59m × 4.38m/141in × 172in), done in 1642, is full of vigour and action, showing the guardsmen poised to march out on patrol rather than drawn up stiffly on parade, as they are in most other portraits of guard companies – such as those works by Joachim von Sandrart (1606–1688) and Bartholomaeus van der Helst (1611–1670) that also appear in this room. Such paintings were routinely commissioned by the commanders of Amsterdam's militia companies. These commanders were rich men – they had to be. Because the commanders were required to arm and uniform their followers out of their own pockets, militia leadership came to be a prestige role which only the well-off could afford. Painting these group portraits for the wealthy company commanders was a steady source of income for the city's artists.

Backtrack briefly to Room 223, which contains background material about the Rembrandt picture, including evidence that when painted it was even bigger: in the early 18th century, some 30cm (1ft) was trimmed from the top and 60cm (2ft) from the left-hand side, apparently to make it fit into the space allocated for it in the Stadhuys on the Dam (now the Royal Palace).

Rembrandt's disciples
The walk back to the foyer from *The Night Watch* is through an arcade of rooms called the Gallery of Honour, where pride of place is usually given to further Rembrandt masterpieces and to other painters of the Rembrandt school. Rembrandt's own *The Jewish Bride* and *The Syndics*, both painted towards the end of his life, are normally hung in Rooms 229 and 230. Other painters usually on display in this gallery include Ferdinand Bol (*c.*1616–1680), Govaert Flinck (1615–1660) and Aert de Gelder (1645–1727), all followers of Rembrandt, plus too many others to list.

The Rijksmuseum's embarrassment of riches by no means ends here, but after *The Night Watch* almost anything else risks seeming anti-climactic. Better to end on a high note, and leave the museum for the wide-open spaces of the Vondelpark.

Amsterdam's greenest space
Turning left as you leave the museum's north side, walk back along Stadhouderskade and turn left again onto Pieter Cornelisz Hooftstraat, which leads directly to one of the entrances to the Vondelpark, a long, 48-hectare (120-acre) rectangle of lawns, trees and lakes slanting southwest from Singelgracht.

Joost van den Vondel was to Dutch poetry and drama what his near contemporary Rembrandt was to painting; indeed, one of the scenes from his towering drama Gijsbrecht van Amstel is claimed to have provided the painter with the inspiration for *The Night Watch*. Like Rembrandt, too, Vondel went from rags to riches and back again, ending his days on a state pension.

The Vondelpark, the largest green space near the city-centre, was landscaped at the end of the 19th century. It is a lively place, especially in summer, when it becomes a magnet attracting sunbathers, kite-fliers, frisbee-throwers, musicians and street entertainers. In the late 1960s and early 1970s it became a mecca for the European counter-culture, with thousands of people camping and creating a summer-long festival atmosphere, but the hippie dream turned sour with an increase in robberies and hard-drug use, so that eventually the police cracked down on people sleeping in the park.

Open-air rock concerts and the impromptu jewellery-sellers who flock here on a summer Sunday give the park an agreeably off-beat atmosphere that is all that remains of the hippie days. Amazingly, the vendors still seem to find a market for the same sort of old tat they were peddling 25 years ago. The Vondelpark summer festival runs between early June and late August and features open-air performances by all sorts of musicians in the Vondelpark Openlucht Theater.

A statue of Vondel by Louis Royer, dated 1867, greets you as you enter the park; he surveys his domain from a pedestal designed by P.J.H. Cuypers and adorned with representations of the Muses of Poetry and Tragedy. Cuypers' elaborate style contrasts strongly with the bizarre building opposite, overlooking the lake. 't Ronde Blauwe Theehouse (Round Blue Teahouse) is a fine specimen of 1930s functionalism. It looks like something from a *Flash Gordon* film set, but is the ideal place for a cup of coffee.

Your route through the park can depend on the weather. On a summer's day, follow the long perimeter loop which winds through the English-style parkland. The sweeps of pathway and woodland are interspersed with eccentrically shaped stretches of water, lined with weeping willows and crossed by toy-like bridges – vistas from a willow-pattern teacup.

Celebrating the movies

Alternatively, walk around the lake, cross it by way of the bandstand on an island close to the entrance, and turn right up the opposite shore to reach the Nederlands Filmmuseum. Designed in 1881 by P.J. Hamer (1812–1887), the museum is a building of contrasts. On the outside it is a pretty 19th-century pavilion, very much in tune with its surroundings; inside it is a picture palace from the first golden age of moving pictures. The interior of the Cinéma Parisien, Amsterdam's first movie theatre, was salvaged from demolition in 1987 and has been painstakingly restored within this building. The museum is at the heart of the increasingly self-confident Netherlands film industry; it presents three screenings of new and classic films every day, plus an ever-changing programme of exhibitions on the development of the cinema.

Leave the Vondelpark by the Filmmuseum Gate and you find yourself at a small oval midway along Vondelstraat. Here the Vondelkerk (Vondel Church) is another of Cuypers's elegant contributions to Amsterdam's architectural heritage. Built in the 1870s, it now houses offices. Turn right here and walk up Vondelstraat, recrossing Stadhouderskade and Singelgracht to the Leidseplein and the end of this walk.

The Plantage and the Artis Zoo

East of the city-centre lies a district of manicured greenery. The Plantage has been a green escape from the intensely urban inner city for at least three centuries. This walk is best enjoyed in summer, and offers the exotic oasis of the Botanical Garden, the adjoining Artis Zoo and a choice of very different museums. One of them is dedicated to children – adults are personae non gratae – so this is an ideal walk if you have the kids with you.

Start/finish:	Waterlooplein; Metro, trams 4, 9, 14
Length:	4.5km (3 miles)
Time:	3hr
Refreshments:	Cafés and restaurants in the Plantage, Artis Zoo and museums
To visit:	● Hortus Botanicus Amsterdam (Botanical Gardens): April 1–October 1, Monday–Friday 09.00–17.00, Saturday–Sunday 11.00–17.00; rest of year Monday–Friday 09.00–16.00, Saturday–Sunday 11.00–16.00
	● National Vakbondsmuseum (National Trades Union Museum): Tuesday–Friday 11.00–17.00, Sunday 13.00–17.00
	● Artis Zoo: daily 09.00–17.00
	● Zoologisch Museum (Zoological Museum): Tuesday–Sunday 09.00–17.00
	● Tropenmuseum (Museum of the Tropics): Monday–Friday 10.00–17.00, Saturday–Sunday 12.00–17.00
	● Kindermuseum (Children's Museum): children 6–12 only, tours on Sundays and public holidays at 12.15, 13.30 and 14.45, reservation essential (tel 5688300)
	● Hollandse Schouwburg: daily 11.00–16.00

Leaving Waterlooplein in a southeasterly direction, walk across Mr Visserplein to Jonas Daniel Meijerplein, the open space named after Amsterdam's first Jewish barrister and the first Jew to gain full citizenship. Meijer (1780–1834) was a doughty fighter for Jewish rights.

The statue in the centre of the square is De Dokwerker (The Dockworker), erected in 1952 as a memorial to the dockers who led a general strike in protest against the rounding-up of Jews which began in February 1941. Quickly and violently broken, the strike was more symbolic than effective, but it was only the first of the many courageous public acts of resistance which continued throughout the years of the German Occupation.

Cross the plein and turn left on Nieuwe Herengracht, then cross the canal by the Hortusbrug (Garden Bridge) to enter the district still called the Plantage (Plantation).

65

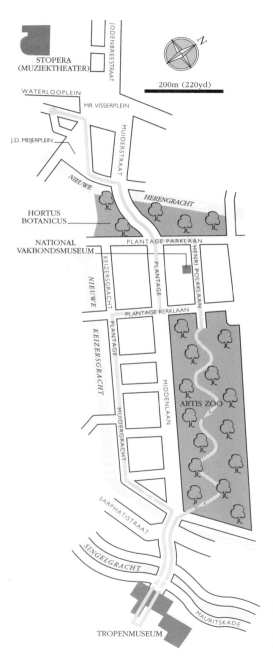

A garden of delight

Amsterdam's explosive growth during its 17th-century Golden Age meant there was no land to spare within the city walls for anything except homes, workshops and warehouses. Even the few courtyards of the city hofjes (almshouses) seem like major concessions in what is still one of the most built-up cities in Europe; the wealthiest merchant princes could afford no more than the tiniest of gardens in the city-centre. Instead, Amsterdammers in search of a green refuge rented patches of land east of the Amstel, some distance from their homes, first as vegetable plots, then as more decorative, recreational gardens. Coffee-shops and teahouses sprang up to cater to the gardeners and to the weekend visitors who strolled out from the city to enjoy the greenery and fresh air. The district came to be known as Amsterdam's 'garden of delight'. By the 19th century, many wealthy families built substantial villas in the region, which also became a centre for the city's diamond industry and one of the focuses of Amsterdam's Jewish community, who provided most of the diamond trade's brokers and skilled artisans.

From the Hortusbrug, bear left to Plantage Middenlaan and the entrance to the Hortus Botanicus (Botanical Gardens), laid out in 1682. The gardens' main purposes were scientific and commercial, allowing Amsterdam's doctors and apothecaries to grow and study medicinal herbs, spices and other plants brought back by Dutch explorers from the ends of the earth. One of the gardens' main sponsors was the Dutch East India Company, which was keen to find new ways of keeping its seamen in good health on long voyages. The horticulturalists also studied new crops and potentially profitable plants – such as coffee, cinnamon, oil palm and pineapple – from Dutch possessions overseas. The coffee plantations of South America had their genesis in the seeds grown here from plants brought back from the East by Dutch sailors.

The gardens are not large, and how much time you spend here will depend on how keen you are on plants, of which there are more than 2000 varieties, but do not miss the medicinal herb garden, the orangery, the monumental palm house and the high-tech tropical greenhouses. Being inside these controlled tropical environments is a bit like being aboard a spaceship. In spring, you can see some of earliest varieties of tulip, and children and other connoisseurs of the bizarre will enjoy the steamy jungle atmosphere of the house where the flesh-eating plants are kept!

A workers' castle

Leaving the Hortus Botanicus, turn left onto Plantage Parklaan, then right onto Henri Polaklaan, passing on your left the oldest small park in the city – the Wertheim Park, a relic of the original Plantage green space – and a monument to the victims of Auschwitz designed by Jan Wolkers. A short distance along Henri Polaklaan, at no. 9, is the Nationaal Vakbondsmuseum (National Trades Union Museum). The collection and displays centre on the history of the Dutch trades union movement and the diamond-cutting industry, but (unless you are a student of such things) the building itself is the real attraction. Known as De Burcht van Berlage (Berlage's Castle), it was commissioned by the General Netherlands Diamond Workers' Union and completed in 1900. The highly skilled diamond workers were in a stronger bargaining position than most other employees, and their union – led by Henri Polak, after whom the street is named – was in the vanguard of the labour movement in the Netherlands. The architect Hendrick Petrus Berlage thought the building was his best, which must have been galling for the arch-capitalists who commissioned him to build the Amsterdam Stock Exchange (see page 20). The splendid staircase, with its decorative brickwork and soaring arches, the grand council room and the boardroom – with fine murals by the Dutch Impressionist painter Roland Holst – are all finely preserved.

Birds and beasts

Walk on down Henri Polaklaan and cross Plantage Kerklaan to the entrance to the Artis Zoo. Founded in 1838, this is the oldest zoo on the European continent, and currently has representatives of 900 animal species plus a wealth of plant life. The zoo's paths are dotted with statues, most of them commemorating obscure Dutch botanists and zoologists. As at the Hortus Botanicus, how long you spend here will depend on how you feel about zoos. The larger animals are in the eastern half of the zoo. A planetarium, geological museum and zoological museum, an aquarium and a children's playground complement the captive animals. The Zoological Museum, housed in the Aquarium Building, has no permanent display but operates a pro-gramme of changing exhibitions. Leave the zoo by the Aquarium Gate, in the southeast corner, to rejoin Plantage Middenlaan.

At the end of this street, a bridge crosses Muidergracht. At the other side, cross Sarphatistraat. Ahead and to your left is a florid 18th-century arch, the Muiderpoort, through which Napoleon made a triumphal entry into the city in 1811.

A visit to the tropics

Walk through this arch, cross a second bridge onto the Mauritskade, and enter the Tropenmuseum (Tropical Museum), housed in an elegant complex of 19th-century buildings. Amsterdam's connection with the tropics goes back all the way to the early years of the Dutch East India Company – some days you can't help wondering if at least part of their outward urge was a desire to escape the cold of the Dutch winter!

Permanent exhibits re-create town and village streets from Asia, Africa, the Arab world, Polynesia and South America, with reconstructed buildings and recorded sounds and sights; all that you are missing are the smells. Also in the building is a Children's Museum, specially targeted at those aged 6–12. It offers a programme of guided tours, for which prior reservation is necessary.

From the Tropenmuseum, retrace your steps to the end of Plantage Middenlaan, then turn left onto Plantage Muidergracht and follow it to its junction with Plantage Kerklaan. At the corner, turn right into Plantage Kerklaan, then left onto Plantage Middenlaan. The pilastered Neoclassical frontage of the Hollandse Schouwburg is immediately on your left, at Plantage Middenlaan 24.

Victims of the Holocaust

Built in 1897, the Schouwburg was used for light opera, then became the main venue for the early-20th-century revival of Dutch drama. During the German Occupation in World War II, the Nazis used it as a concentration point for Dutch Jews. From here the prisoners were sent to the transit camp at Westerbork, then to the death camps of Sobibor and Auschwitz. Since the 1960s the empty façade of the theatre has been kept as a ghostly memorial to the victims of the Holocaust. The restored part of the museum behind that façade includes an exhibition room with videos and documents from the era of the Nazi Occupation and the deportations. Behind the building is a memorial garden.

Continue along Plantage Middenlaan to no. 4A, the Filmtheater Desmet, a striking Art Deco building which has been in the forefront of Dutch film-making since the end of the last century, and which premieres the latest art movies; Sunday afternoons often offer an opportunity to talk to the directors and producers of new Dutch films and television series.

Follow Plantage Middenlaan back across Nieuwe Herengracht, via the Hortusbrug, and cross Mr Visserplein to return to Waterlooplein and its public transport.

Oosterdok: The East Harbour

Amsterdam turns its back firmly on the open waters of the Ij, its highway to the sea, which is hidden away behind the red-brick battlements of Amsterdam Centraal Station. This walk rectifies that by taking you on a tour of the city's maritime heritage; it includes a ferry trip across the broad waters of the harbour.

Start/finish:	Stationsplein; Metro, all trams and buses
Length:	7km (4.5 miles)
Time:	3hr
Refreshments:	Café/restaurant in Netherlands Maritime Museum; otherwise establishments in Damrak/Prins Hendrikkade area at start or finish
Which day:	Not Mondays; if you want to take the ferry trip, do not go at the weekend
To visit:	● Open Haven Museum: Tuesday–Saturday 10.00–17.00, Sunday 12.00–17.00
	● Werf 't Kromhout: Monday–Friday 10.00–16.00
	● Nederlands Scheepvaarts Museum (Netherlands Maritime Museum): Monday (14 June–13 September only) 10.00–17.00, Tuesday–Saturday 10.00–17.00, Sunday 12.00–17.00

Leave the Stationsplein from its east end, walk past the Amsterdam Tourist Office building and turn right to cross the bridge onto Prins Hendrikkade. The Open Haven – the inner harbour between Stationsplein and Prins Hendrikkade – is a mere shadow of its former bustling self, when cranes and stevedores worked full-time discharging cargoes from the ships of the KNSM (Royal Dutch Steamship Company) and fur-coated, top-hatted passengers transferred with their trunks from the luxury transatlantic liners to the transcontinental express trains leaving from the Centraal Station for the capitals of Europe. The Open Haven Museum, at no. 311 KNSM Laan, was built as the headquarters of the KNSM. Its 19th-century premises now house a wide range of exhibitions, many of them on maritime themes.

A monument to the sea

Cross to the south side of the Open Haven, turn left, and walk along Prins Hendrikkade to the junction with Binnenkant and the whimsical Scheepvaarthuis. You can't miss it: next to the dour, functional warehouse architecture which dominates this section of the quay, it stands out a mile. Built in 1916, it housed the offices of the six biggest Dutch shipping lines; it is now the office of the city transport authority. The exterior of the building is encrusted with statuary – a triumphant, trident-brandishing Neptune is flanked by celebrated admirals, sea creatures, maritime paraphernalia and female figures symbolizing the north, south, east and west. It is a sort of triumphal monument to the Dutch victory over the sea, turning it from a potent adversary into a military ally and a valuable source of trade and wealth.

Among the building's designers were Pieter Kramer (1881–1961) and Michel de Klerk (1884–1923), maverick architects who set out, with their radical new notions, to shake Amsterdam's builders from their dull complacency. They went on to design a number of public buildings and housing projects which dominate the Nieuw Zuid (New South) district south of the River Amstel – buildings which departed so far from Amsterdam's bourgeois traditions that people were initially reluctant to live in them; indeed they do still sit uneasily with the city's older buildings.

Opposite the Scheepvaarthuis is a statue of Prins Hendrik (1820–1879). Nicknamed 'The Sailor Prince', Hendrik took a great interest in the Dutch Merchant Navy, helping to revive flagging 19th-century Amsterdam's pride in its seafaring prowess. The boulevard named after him is now the city's main east–west traffic artery, which makes it an uninspiring route for walkers. Escape it by turning right, past the Scheepvaarthuis, along the quiet waters of the Waals Eilandsgracht. This inner harbour dates from 1644, when the city's booming sea-trade demanded more quays for both river barges and sea-going vessels. Many merchants chose to live here, where they could keep a close eye on business and their ships.

Walk along the quay to the landmark of the Montelbaanstoren, with its dandified spire by Hendrik de Keyser (for more details on the Montelbaanstoren see page 30). Opposite the tower, where the Binnenkant joins the Oude Schans, turn left onto the Kalkmarkt, cross the Oude Schans to your right by the heavily traffic-laden road bridge, and turn right onto 's Gravenhekje, passing the 17th-century waterhouses that once belonged to the West India Company. At the end of this short quay, turn left past the Peperbrug, walking through the heart of one of the old dockside warehouse districts, and go along Rapenburg to one of the oldest taverns in the city.

Café de Druif

It is claimed that Café de Druif ('the Grape'), at no. 83, opened in 1631, and local legend has it that Piet Heyn (1578–1629), the naval hero of the Dutch wars of independence, was a regular. Heyn – who struck a telling blow for the Netherlands by capturing the Spanish silver fleet in 1628, making it impossible for the Spanish generals to pay or feed their discontented troops – certainly lived at no. 13, but it seems unlikely he ever dropped in here for a borrel of geniever; he died two years before Café de Druif opened, and is buried in the Oude Kerk in Delft alongside another famous admiral, Maerten Tromp (1597–1653). If you are setting off round the harbour on a winter day, though, you might want to fortify yourself with a warming drop before continuing.

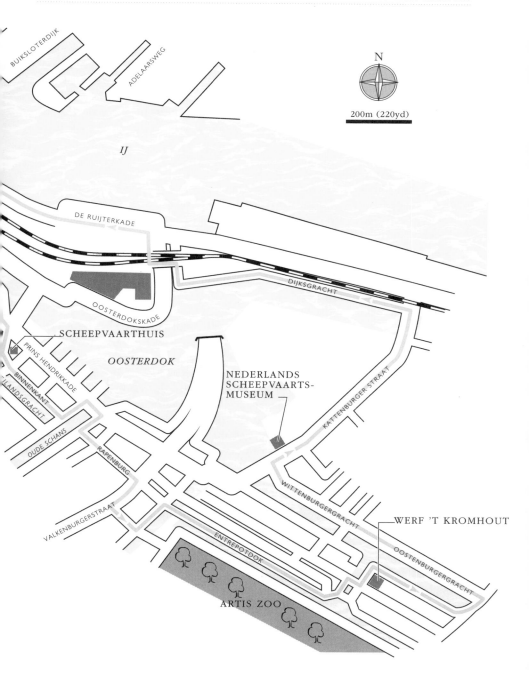

N

200m (220yd)

BUIKSLOTERDIJK

ADELAARSWEG

IJ

DE RUIJTERKADE

DIJKSGRACHT

OOSTERDOKSKADE

SCHEEPVAARTHUIS

OOSTERDOK

PRINS HENDRIKKADE

BINNENKANT

LANDSGRACHT

OUDE SCHANS

RAPENBURG

VALKENBURGERSTRAAT

NEDERLANDS
SCHEEPVAARTS-
MUSEUM

KATTENBURGER STRAAT

WITTENBURGERGRACHT

WERF 'T KROMHOUT

OOSTENBURGERGRACHT

ENTREPOTDOK

ARTIS ZOO

At the end of Rapenburg, turn right on Valkenburgerstraat, left on Anne Frankstraat, and left again on Nieuwe Herengracht. A right turn across a short swing bridge brings you to the entrance of the Entrepotdok, where a long quayside of bonded warehouses – in its day the largest in Europe – has been converted into expensive and sought-after apartments. An indoor arcade runs through the middle of the complex, reached by the Binnenkadijk stairs. With no traffic and a view of the greenery of the Artis Zoo on the far side of the dock, it looks like an enviable place to live.

Engines and windmills
Go about two-thirds of the way along the Entrepotdok and follow the quayside round to your left. Cross a bridge on your right to the Werf 't Kromhout (Kromhout Wharf Museum). The wharf dates from the 18th century and weathered Amsterdam's 19th-century shipbuilding slump to become one of the city's most advanced dockyards. By the early 20th century it was building and fitting diesel engines, which equipped most of the country's vast fleet of canal barges. It is still a working wharf, but the ranks of oily diesel engines which form the bulk of the museum's exhibits will excite only serious engine fans.

From the Kromhout Wharf Museum, turn right and walk along the waterfront of the Nieuwevaart for a closer look at the last windmill close to the city-centre. Contemporary tax records tell us that some 140 windmills were in use in 1765, but today only a handful survive. Windmills are first mentioned in Amsterdam's records as early as 1307, and provided power not only to pump the polders dry but to grind grain, saw wood and run many other industrial processes. As windmill design grew more sophisticated, their sails were designed to set themselves automatically against the wind, using a principle still employed by ocean-going yachts. Wind power was gradually supplanted by steam, then by diesel, though Dutch engineers have helped pioneer the use of high-tech wind generators as a 'green' source of electrical power. The De Gooier windmill – the one in front of you – was built in 1814; it no longer works, but it makes a pretty postcard picture.

Cross the bridge at the corner of Sarphatistraat and Hoogtekadijk and at the other end turn left onto Oostenburgergracht, which runs along the bottoms of the Eastern Islands – Oostenburg, Wittenburg and Kattenburg – which protect the inner harbour. Here, in 1825, the entrepreneur Paul van Vlissingen dragged Amsterdam out of its early-19th-century doldrums and into the age of steam, building an engineering works and opening a steamship line which plied to London and Hamburg. Walk along the waterfront which now connects the three islands. Oostenburgergracht becomes Wittenburgergracht, which in turn becomes Kattenburgergracht. At the end of the waterfront, cross Kattenburgerstraat to visit the prominent Nederlands Scheepvaarts Museum (Netherlands Maritime Museum), at Kattenburgerplein no. 1, which offers a combination of indoor and outdoor exhibits.

Plate 17: *The view from the town hall, overlooking canals and the Inner Amstel (see the Markets and the Amstel walk, page 47).*

Plate 18: *Swift and silent, trams have right of way over all traffic except bicycles – so watch your step!*

Plate 19: The Binnenhof dates from as early as the 13th century (see the Hague 1: Historic buildings walk, page 82).

Plate 20: Antiques of all shapes and sizes are on sale at the Lange Voorhout street market (see the Hague 2: Art, antiques and parks walk, pages 89–90).

Plate 21: *Scheveningen's fine North Sea beach attracts thousands of bathers. Overlooking the beach is the splendid Kurhaus, now a luxury hotel (see the Scheveningen walk, page 98).*

Plate 22: *Designed by Piet Blom, the Blaak Heights 'pole houses' are anything but ordinary (see the Rotterdam 1: Weema to the Maas walk, page 103).*

Plate 23: *War memorial to Rotterdam's dead. The city suffered heavy bombing by both sides during World War II (see the Rotterdam 2: Parks and museums walk, page 107).*

Plate 24: *The St Bavokerk organ, built by famous Amsterdam organ-maker Christian Muller in 1738, is one of the largest in the world (see the Haarlem 1: The Grote Markt and Flemish Haarlem walk, page 114).*

Square-riggers and spices

The museum building dates from 1655, and was originally a Dutch Admiralty warehouse. Its main attraction is the square-rigger *Amsterdam*, a replica of an 18th-century Dutch East Indiaman. Go aboard and try to imagine how squalid conditions must have been below-decks for the crew of 200, who were cooped up here on voyages which stretched into many months (when they weren't scrambling about the giddy heights of the rigging above-deck!). Even for the ordinary sailor, though, the rewards of a trip to the East – to Dutch possessions in southern Africa, Mauritius, Ceylon, India, the Malay peninsula or the East Indies – could be substantial, as he was allowed to engage in small-scale trading in exotic curios on his own account. Not, however, on the original *Amsterdam*, which sank in 1749 on its maiden voyage. In summer, the vessel is crewed by volunteer 'sailors' who re-create life at sea – shaping a course, swabbing the decks, cooking an authentically unappealing shipboard meal, firing off cannon and conducting a sea-burial, while on the quayside you can watch traditional sailmakers and boatbuilders at work.

In 1995, the *Amsterdam* was joined by the *Batavia*, a replica of another East Indiaman which in 1629 likewise sank on what was its maiden voyage to the Orient. The *Batavia* was the flagship of a flotilla of seven ships which, under the command of Captain François Pelsaert, set out from Amsterdam in October 1628 on one of the first expeditions to Australia.

For more than 20 years, Dutch captains had been returning from the East Indies with word of a vast new continent lying far south of Java. India and the East Indies had proved unimaginably wealthy, and the Dutch East India Company hoped for even greater wealth from this undiscovered land. Pelsaert's mission was to establish trade links with the supposed princes of the new kingdoms, and his ships carried gold, jewels and mechanical toys as gifts. They never made it. Instead, the *Batavia* was wrecked on the Abrolhos Shoals, off the west coast of Australia. Leaving 200 survivors of the wreck marooned on a desert island, Pelsaert set out in an open boat on a 1900-km (1200-mile) journey to Batavia, the chief settlement of the Dutch East Indies, to bring help. After a month-long voyage, he arrived at the settlement; but when he came back to the Abrolhos Shoals aboard the vessel *Sardam* to rescue the survivors he found that more than half of them had been murdered by mutineers. Pelsaert hanged two of the ringleaders and marooned two more on the desert mainland. Ironically, his epic journey to Batavia and back provided the first detailed maps and reports of Australia, and at the same time discouraged the VOC's directors from further expeditions to a land which showed no opportunities for profitable trade. From the quayside you can visit the museum's Multimedia Theatre, where sound and video images re-create the long sea voyage to Batavia – now Jakarta.

Other high points of the museum include a re-creation of the vanished world of the great luxury passenger liners which – until air travel put them out of business in the 1960s – sailed regularly across the Atlantic and Indian oceans. There are also a lavishly decorated royal barge, once used for waterborne processions around the canals on occasions of state, and a room dedicated to the tribulations of the Dutch Merchant Navy during World War II.

The grisliest relic on display, beyond doubt, is a glass bell-jar containing a pickled grey piece of skin and flesh which is all that remains of Lieutenant Jan van Speyk of the Netherlands Navy, who in a spectacular display of Dutch obstinacy blew up his own vessel in Antwerp Harbour rather than surrender it to the rebels during the Belgian Uprising of 1831.

Turn left as you come out of the museum and walk north along Kattenburgerstraat, the main street of this once fiercely insular working-class district. Cross Dijksgracht, then go under the railway bridge. Facing you – across the traffic-laden Piet Heinkade, named after the 17th-century admiral, and Oostelijke Handelskade – are the waters of the Ijhaven, an arm of the Ij, Amsterdam's highway to the sea, with the cranes and warehouses of North Amsterdam on the other side. The waterfront here is uninspiring, so turn left and walk briskly back along Piet Heinkade and De Ruijterkade towards Centraal Station. The final stretch of this rather dull waterfront road is named after Admiral Michael de Ruyter (1607–1676): the scourge of the Netherlands' enemies at sea for a generation.

Across the Ij

This walk finishes with a short boat journey, the best way of enjoying a vista of the harbour, the Ij and the city waterfront. Returning to Stationsplein, walk behind the Centraal Station building to the Ij waterfront, the oldest part of the port of Amsterdam. Once a bay of the inland Zuiderzee (now mostly reclaimed and known as the Ijsselmeer), the Ij was the cradle of the city's sea power; until the 17th century even the largest sailing vessels could cross the Zuiderzee to reach the North Sea, but navigation became increasingly difficult as the inland waters silted up and vessels grew larger. In 1872 work began on the North Sea Channel, connecting the port of Amsterdam directly with the open sea. Completed in 1876, it was one of the greatest works of marine engineering ever attempted.

Continue along De Ruijterkade, behind the station, to Pont nar Tolhuis and its landing stages for a free round trip to the north side and a fine view of the harbour and its shipping. There is no better symbol of the relationship between Amsterdam and the sea: the two vast harbour basins and the dock islands with their 40km (25 miles) of quayside are entirely man-made. Take the small Ij–Veer ferry (Monday–Friday only) from landing stage no. 8 to North Amsterdam's eastern ferry pier at Meeuwenlaan. On dry land again, walk up Meeuwenlaan and bear left along Adelaarsweg towards the Noord Hollandsch Kanaal (North Holland Canal) and its lock. Cross the canal at the lock, turn left on Buiksloterweg, and walk down to the Buiksloterwegveer ferry pier. The free ferry makes the trip to landing stage no. 8 on the other side, behind Centraal Station, eight times hourly between 06.30 and 21.00.

Westelijk Eilanden (The Western Islands)

Though they sound romantically remote, the Western Islands are in fact a stone's throw from the centre, though until quite recently they were — like the three islands which guard the Eastern Dock — the core of a close-knit dockland community and a law unto themselves. If you are looking for the 'real Amsterdam', look no further: here you'll find pretty houses, modern apartments, rafts of houseboats, artists' collectives and graffiti-covered walls. It is a part of the city that tourism hasn't yet got at, and it is full of character.

Start:	Haarlemmerplein; trams 3, 18, 22
Finish:	Centraal Station; Metro, all buses and trams
Length:	3.2km (2 miles)
Time:	1hr
Refreshments:	Scarce on the route, but there are cafés at Haarlemmerplein, for before you set out, and around the Centraal Station area, for after you've finished
Which day:	Any day
To visit:	● Amsterdam Beeldhouwers Kolektief (Amsterdam Sculptors' Collective): Wednesday–Sunday 13.00–18.00

Your landmark on Haarlemmerplein, a busy traffic junction at the northwest corner of the Jordaan district, is a florid triumphal gateway built for the coronation of King William II in 1840, following the abdication of his father William I.

Earlier heads of state named William had technically been Stadhouders, a title for which there is no good English translation. They were appointed by an electoral college and did not hold royal title; in practice, however, the princes of the House of Orange, descendants of William the Silent, were always elected. Conspicuous and pompous, the arch occupies most of the west side of the square.

Keeping the gateway on your left, leave Haarlemmerplein by its north side, cross Haarlemmer Houttuinen to Nieuwe Teertuinen, and turn right to cross the Galgenbrug (Gallows Bridge), so arriving on Prinseneiland. The painter George Breitner (1857–1923), a contemporary and friend of Van Gogh, had his studio nearby, and the rough and ready dockside underworld of this district provided him with inspiration for many of his paintings.

The Princes' Island

Prinseneiland (Princes' Island), like its neighbours, is an artificial island, dredged in the 17th century out of what is now the Westerdok to provide more space for warehouses and merchants' homes and for their ships to anchor conveniently alongside. One of the biggest and wealthiest of these warehouses, the Huys de Drie Prinsen (House of the Three Princes), was decorated with busts of three Princes of

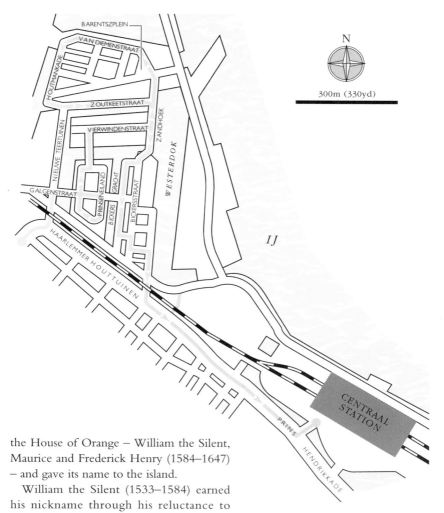

the House of Orange – William the Silent,
Maurice and Frederick Henry (1584–1647)
– and gave its name to the island.

William the Silent (1533–1584) earned
his nickname through his reluctance to
come out for the Protestant cause until 1568, when he led the first campaign against
the Spanish Duke of Alva, beginning the Eighty Years' War against Spain. Ten years
later his rebel army and fleet had driven the Spaniards out of the Netherlands –
Amsterdam was the last city to surrender to him – and he was chosen by the States-
General (the governing council) as the new Dutch Republic's first Stadhouder. He
was assassinated in 1584, and was succeeded as Stadhouder by his son Maurice
(Maurits) of Nassau (1567–1625), one of the finest and most feared generals in 16th-
century Europe. Forging an army which dealt a series of crushing defeats to Spain, he

forced the Spaniards to recognize Dutch independence and sign the Twelve Years' Truce in 1609.

From the end of the bridge, carry straight on along Galgenstraat and turn right. You'll find a row of imposing warehouses along the quayside (also called Prinseneiland), which forms the eastern side of the island. Amsterdam's first merchants simply stashed their wares in the attics of their own homes. Like the warehouses, most older buildings still have a strong beam projecting from the gable end, used to haul goods up from the canal or street-level to the attic – and still routinely employed to haul large items of furniture which won't fit through the narrow doors and stairways of most older homes.

Lanes and warehouses

To get the full flavour of Prinseneiland, devote half an hour or so to walking around the island, sampling the waterfront and narrow lanes in the middle of the island where gentrification is beginning to transform the district from dockland to trendy suburb. Naturally the most desirable properties are those by the water's edge, and more and more of the old warehouses are being turned into attractive apartments. Finally, head for the bridge on the northern side of Prinseneiland and cross it to arrive on Realengracht, the southern side of Realeneiland. Walk straight on across the tiny island, and turn right when you reach Vierwindenstraat, which parallels the waterfront on its northern shore.

A golden pun

At the far (eastern) end of the row of 17th-century houses overlooking the canal is De Goudene Real, home of the merchant after whom the island is named. Now a small restaurant, it is easy to identify by the gold coin on its gablestone. Like many gable images, this is quite a complicated visual pun on the owner's name and his loyalties. The householder was one Jacob Real, a prominent trader. A real was also a gold coin, minted by the kings of Spain. Real himself was a Catholic, and therefore may have felt some sympathy for the Catholic Spanish monarchy; the gold coin on his gable was a way of discreetly announcing his royalist leanings without being so flagrant as to bring the wrath of the authorities down on him.

Turn left on Zandhoek, a quayside of late-17th-century homes running alongside Westerdok harbour. Rocking at anchor sit a dozen or more fine old sailing barges. On a sunny summer afternoon this looks like a very attractive place to live by the water; on a wintry day, however, you may not be so envious of the owners.

At the north end of Zandhoek, curve away from the harbour, to your left, and cross the nondescript Barentszplein to turn left on Van Diemenstraat, named after Antony Van Diemen (1593–1645), Governor-General of the Dutch East Indies in the 1630s and 1640s. Van Diemen's biggest claim to fame is his sponsorship of an able young navigator named Abel Janszoon Tasman (1603–c.1659), whose voyage of discovery in 1642–3 proved for the first time that Australia was a vast island, not part of a still greater southern continent. The modest Tasman, discovering a large island to the southeast of Australia, named it after his patron. During the 18th century Van Diemen's Land came to have an evil reputation as a British prison colony. In 1835 more respectable British settlers renamed it Tasmania; so poor old Van Diemen has no memorial but this windy, north-facing quayside on the Ij. Tasman's discoveries – which included also New Zealand – are shown on a splendid map inlaid in mosaic on the floor of the Royal Palace in Amsterdam.

Return along Houtmankade and Zoutkeetstraat to Zandhoek and retrace your steps to the dinky white bridge that connects Realeneiland with Bickerseiland.

A fleet of houseboats and a herd of goats

Like its neighbour, Bickerseiland is named after the wealthy local merchant who was prominent among its first settlers. Anchored along the quay is one of Amsterdam's biggest fleets of houseboats (there are more than 2400 in the whole city). Some are luxurious purpose-built jobs, while others are haywire conversions, originally canal or sea-going barges, pontoons or tugboats. It seems that Amsterdam's canal-dwellers will set up home on anything that floats.

Bickerseiland is no longer a shipyard, but some of its street-names carry memories of the old days, like Zeilmakerstraat (Sailmaker Street), a picturesque name for a now undistinguished street. The island is covered with functional apartment blocks – with one surprising exception. Midway along Bickersgracht, and a little way inland, keep your ears open for the sounds of chickens clucking and goats bleating. A tiny farmyard sits incongruously among the blocks of flats, with a small herd of goats, plus poultry and hutches full of rabbits.

Walk along Bickersgracht, the inner waterfront opposite Prinseneiland, and turn left onto Minnemoerstraat; go down Bickersstraat, to your right, towards the Westerdok. Turn left into Zeilmakerstraat; housed in an older building at no. 15 Zeilmakerstraat is the Amsterdam Beeldhouwers Kolektief (Sculptors' Collective), a grouping of more than 50 sculptors whose work is exhibited here. Works on display are constantly changing, and most are for sale.

Turn right along Hollandse Tuin and walk by the dockside. Pass beneath the main railway line (there are some fine examples of the latest in spray-can graffiti art on the bridge arches), and turn left on Haarlemmer Houttuinen to walk back, via Prins Hendrikkade, to Amsterdam Centraal Station.

AROUND AMSTERDAM:
THE RANDSTADT TOWNS

A msterdam's orbital towns and cities are the homes of some four million people – over one-quarter of the Dutch population. This conurbation, known as the Randstadt (the Round City), contains three major cities – Den Haag (The Hague), Rotterdam, and Utrecht – interspersed with smaller towns. The most interesting of these – Delft, Gouda, Leiden and Haarlem – have plenty to offer walkers.

This region is the historic heart of Holland, and each town and city is packed with mementoes of the country's statesmen, artists and architects, inventors and musicians, and of the ebb and flow of the fortunes of the Netherlands over centuries. None is more than an hour away from Amsterdam by train; each has its own distinct character and attractions, and each is well worth a day or a half-day trip from the city.

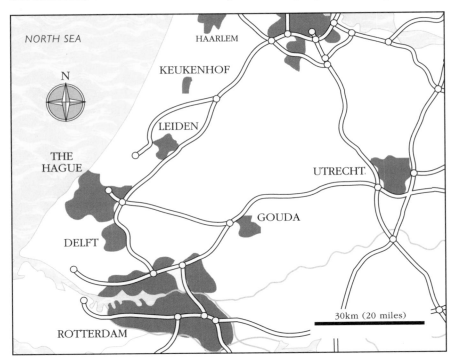

The Hague 1: Historic buildings

Den Haag (The Hague) is the formal capital of the Netherlands and the seat of government (although it is in Amsterdam that the country's monarchs are crowned). It became a royal residence in 1248, when William (1228–1256), Count of Holland, built a castle here. In the 16th century it became the first capital of the newly independent United Provinces of the Netherlands. Today it is an international and cosmopolitan city, the site of the World Court. This walk features The Hague's grand royal and official palaces as well as medieval churches and castles, almshouses and one of the world's finest collections of Dutch paintings.

Start/finish:	Den Haag Hollands Spoor Station; trams 8, 9, 11, 12; trains to and from Amsterdam Centraal Station go 4–6 times hourly and take about 45 minutes
Length:	6.5km (4 miles)
Time:	3hr
Refreshments:	Restaurants and cafés throughout the old centre, in most museums, and in Hoogstraat and the indoor arcades at Hofweg
Which day:	Not Sunday
To visit:	● Mauritshuis (Royal Collection of Paintings): Tuesday–Saturday 10.00–17.00, Sunday 11.00–17.00
	● Binnenhof Ridderzaal: guided tours Monday–Saturday 10.00–16.00 when possible
	● Schildergallerij Prins Willem V: Tuesday–Saturday 10.00–17.00, Sunday 11.00–17.00
	● Gevangenpoort (Prison Gate) Museum: Tuesday–Friday 11.00–17.00, Saturday–Sunday 12.00–17.00
	● Dutch Games of Chance Museum: Monday–Friday 09.00–16.00
	● Museum Bredius: Tuesday–Saturday 10.00–17.00, Sunday 11.00–17.00
	● Historic Museum of The Hague: Tuesday–Saturday 10.00–17.00, Sunday 11.00–17.00
	● Lange Voorhout Palace Museum: Tuesday–Saturday 10.00–17.00, Sunday 11.00–17.00

Starting from the Hollands Spoor Station, turn left onto the Spui and walk up to the junction with Herengracht. Herengracht takes a kink to the left, then to the right where it joins Korte Poten. Continue along Korte Poten to its junction with the Plein, and turn right. This spacious square, ringed by lime trees, was once the kitchen garden of the royal court, and is surrounded by dignified state buildings. In the centre of the square is a statue of William I, cast by Louis Royer in 1848.

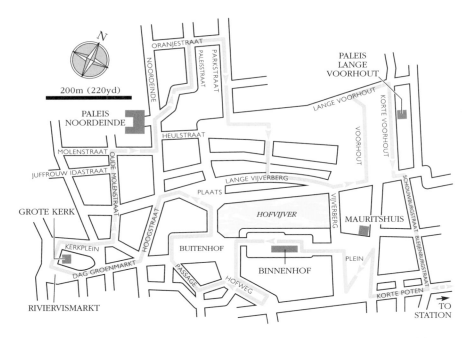

On your right as you walk up the side of the square, at no. 23, is an elaborate building in Louis XIV style, bearing the triple-saltire coat-of-arms of the city of Amsterdam; this was originally the residence of Amsterdam's representatives to the States-General, the Dutch Parliament, which was located in The Hague. In the 19th century it became a royal residence, and it is now the headquarters of the Office for Visual Arts. A little further along, on the opposite side of the street, the De Witte Building, an entertaining long building in the eclectic neo-Renaissance style, has a chequered history. The De Witte Literary Society's first building – the right-hand wing of the existing block – was designed in 1870 by Cornelijs Outshoorn (1810–1875). Other architects added a centre section and a left-hand wing in the same style, in 1899, and a still later corner section was added in 1930.

Cut diagonally from the De Witte building across the Plein to its south corner. At Plein no. 2, the new Lower House of the Dutch Lower House, designed by P.I. de Bruijn and completed in 1992, bears a remarkable resemblance to Star Trek's spaceship *Enterprise*. For contrast, look at the austere sandstone façade of the Ministry of Defence, at no. 4 Plein. It carries the Rotterdam city coat-of-arms and was originally the residence of Rotterdam's delegation to the States-General, built between 1739 and 1746.

At nos. 2A and 2B, the offices of the CDA (Christian Democrat Party) are in a fine example of Dutch neo-Renaissance architecture, built in 1883 and designed by C.H.

Peters (1847–1932). The elaborate stucco building beside it displays the lighter touch of an earlier government architect, W.N. Rose, and was built in 1861 as the Ministry of Colonial Affairs; it is now the headquarters of another political party, the PVDA (Popular Free Democrats).

The Sugar Palace

The final stop on the Plein is at its northeast: the Mauritshuis, a delightful Baroque building at the corner of the square and Korte Vijverberg. Designed by Jacob van Campen and completed in 1644, this is one of the first and finest examples of Dutch Classical Baroque. Its façade is, typically, decorated with pilasters and embellished by a pediment decorated by sculptures. The building is nicknamed the Sugar Palace for its builder, Count Johan Maurits of Nassau (1604–1679), Governor of the newly conquered province of Dutch Brazil. The Dutch had seized this territory (now independent Suriname in South America) from the Portuguese after the end of the Twelve Years' Truce in 1621. Johan Maurits used his time as Governor to make a fortune in the sugar trade.

Damaged by fire in 1704, the building was given a new interior in 18th-century style, and since 1822 has been the home of the Royal Collection of Paintings, one of the finest collections of old Dutch masters in the world. Its treasury of 300 works includes the world's largest collection of Rembrandts, plus paintings by Frans Hals, Peter Paul Rubens (1577–1640) and Jan Vermeer. Highlights of the Rembrandt collection include *The Anatomy Lesson*, painted when he was 26, and a quartet of self-portraits which span four decades of the painter's life. In the first, the jauntily dressed Rembrandt wears a plumed velvet hat; gold earrings dangle from his ears, and he is clearly on top of the world. The last shows him as a jowly, disillusioned old man. Even when painting himself, Rembrandt had a cynic's eye for character and an inability to flatter. Another of the museum's prizes is *Young Bull* by Paulus Potter (1625–1654), a vast – 2.2m × 3.3m (7ft × 11ft) – rural scene which glows with life. Frans Hals is represented by a series of portraits and Vermeer by three paintings, finest of which is *A View of Delft*, which looks as fresh as if it had been painted yesterday.

Medieval splendour

From the Mauritshuis, turn your back on the Plein and prepare to enter the magnificent Binnenhof. The oldest parts of this truly splendid complex date from the 13th century, when Count Floris V (1254–1296) built a moated castle here. In 1585 it became the seat of the States-General of the United Provinces, which was the first independent government of the Netherlands.

Enter the Binnenhof through the Grenadier's Gate. On your right a long neo-Renaissance building houses the Ministry of Public Affairs. It is one of the most recent parts of the complex, built in 1913 but incorporating older elements such as the Louis XIV-style Treveszaal (Hall of Treves) and an octagonal 15th-century turret which is now the Prime Minister's office; he has a fine view looking out over the Hofvijver, the decorative lake which runs along the north side of the Binnenhof.

Immediately ahead of you is the oldest part of the building, the 13th-century castle. The wooden dome which crowns it is a century-old copy of the original, which was torn down in 1861. Within, the Ridderzaal (Knights' Hall) – a magnificent hall, 38m (118ft) long, supported by delicate Gothic arches – is used for the opening of Parliament in September, when the Queen arrives by state coach, attended by liveried footmen, to make her annual speech.

Enter the Binnenhof Visitors' Centre, in the vaults of the Ridderzaal, by the doorway at no. 8A Binnenhof. Here you can enjoy a presentation on the history of the complex. Guided tours leave from here throughout the year.

Within the castle building and behind the Ridderzaal is the equally antiquated Rolzaal (Hall of the Rolls), once the courtroom of the Dutch Supreme Council and High Court.

Walk on through the Binnenhof. On your left as you reach the rear of the castle is the former hall of the Lower House, built in the style of Louis XVI as a ballroom in 1793. On your right is the Upper House, where the States-General originally convened, built in 1652–57. It retains its Baroque interior, with painted wooden cove ceilings and Renaissance arched galleries. Immediately ahead, the Binnenhof Fountain, built in 1885, is the work of P.J.H. Cuypers, architect of Amsterdam's Centraal Station and Rijksmuseum. A gilded statue atop the fountain represents King William II; gargoyles decorate the cast-iron stem.

Leave the Binnenhof by the Stadhouderspoort (Stadhouder's Gate). Traditionally, use of this gateway connecting the Binnenhof with the outer Buitenhof was restricted to the Stadhouder and his attendants except on May Day, when the people of The Hague were allowed into the Binnenhof to dance around the maypole.

Royal shopping

Turn left, walk along Hofweg, then cross the street to the corner of Hofweg and Spuistraat. The imposing building in front of you is Meddens, the work of another ground-breaking Amsterdam architect, H.P. Berlage, but the giant rams' heads beneath the pediment cornices are the contribution of his assistant, Lambertus Zijl. The frieze along the eaves depicts the story of St Martin, the Roman centurion who gave his cloak to a shivering beggar. Meddens is The Hague's answer to Harrods, an aristocratic fashion house with a long pedigree and the right to call itself a 'royal shop' as supplier to the Dutch Royal Family.

For a different kind of shopping, turn left into the Passage, a lavish indoor shopping arcade with a domed glass roof, palm trees and fashionable stores. Two neo-Renaissance wings, both dating from 1882, lead one to the Spuistraat and the other to the Buitenhof. A third wing, built in the Expressionist style of the 1920s, leads to the Hofweg. Follow the Buitenhof wing and turn right.

In the Middle Ages this forecourt of the Count's palace was linked by narrow alleys to the small village of Die Haeghe, later to grow into The Hague. It became a more open space in the 18th and 19th centuries, with the building of new city streets on all sides. On the corner of the inner square and the outer Buitenhof, at no. 35, is the Schildergallerij Prins Willem V (Prince William V Painters' Gallery). Built in 1774, it housed the Stadhouder's private collection until the French Occupation of the Napoleonic era, when the paintings were spirited off to the Louvre. On their return to The Hague they were transferred to the Mauritshuis. While what remains is worth a look and the building itself is attractive, there is no doubt that the Mauritshuis got the best of the paintings once displayed here.

A grim prison

Next door, at no. 33, is the Gevangenpoort (Prison Gate) Museum. The massive arched gate-tower once guarded the outer portal of the Binnenhof, and from about 1420 the counts of Holland used it as a jail. In 1828 the prison moved to new and (one hopes) less grim premises, and in 1882 the gate-tower became a national museum exhibiting grisly instruments of torture. Their uses are explained in rather more detail than you may wish to know. Through the gateway, in the Plaats beyond, you can see a bronze statue of one of the prison's victims, the statesman Johan De Witt (1625–1672). Imprisoned here for their radical views in 1672, he and his brother Cornelis (1629–1672) were dragged from their cell by a mob and murdered.

Turn left into the Plaats, cross to where it narrows into Hoogstraat, and walk down Hoogstraat to the corner of the Dagelijkse Groenmarkt and Grote Halstraat. On the corner, the inn called 't Goude Hooft (The Golden Hat) has been on this site since medieval times, though the present building dates from the 17th century and was restored in the 1930s. Its interior, in the style of the Delft School, is well preserved, with a wooden minstrels' gallery overlooking the main hall.

Nobles and commoners

Walk along the Dagelijkse Groenmarkt to the Oude Stadhuis (Old Town Hall), built in Flemish–Dutch Renaissance style in 1565. During and after the Middle Ages, The Hague was really two communities: the Binnenhof, surrounded by the homes of the wealthy along the Hofvijver and the Lange Voorhout, and the village of Die Heaghe, where the ordinary folk lived around their Grote Kerk and Town Hall. With its richly decorated façade, the Stadhuis – built on the foundations of an earlier building, the medieval Hof van Brederode – is one of the earliest Renaissance buildings in the northern Netherlands. Atop the façade is the city coat-of-arms, a stork representing justice and discretion. Above is a Latin proverb: Ne Jupiter Quidem Omnibus (Even Jupiter cannot please everyone). Take a look inside at the opulent interior decor of the hall's surviving 16th- and 17th-century rooms before carrying on along the Dagelijkse Groenmarkt to the Grote Kerk (St Jacob's Church).

Rebuilt after a fire in 1539, the church, beside the Oude Stadhuis, has since been repeatedly restored and altered. In 1956 the upper section of its unusual octagonal neo-Gothic cast-iron spire was replaced by a wooden replica of the 16th-century spire. The nave of the church is marked by a series of gables and the upper choir by a distinctive railing and roof-turret. The Grote Kerk is a treasury of 16th-century craftsmanship. The Renaissance pulpit dates from 1550; the walls bear scutcheons of King Philip the Good (1396–1467), Duke of Burgundy, and his Knights of the Golden Fleece; and two rich stained-glass windows are attributed to the mid-16th-century artist Dirck Crabeth. The carillon in the belfry was cast by Melchior de Haze of Antwerp in 1686, and the great Jesus bell, largest of three tolling bells, by the foundrymen Jaspar and Jan Moer in 1541.

At the end of Riviervismarkt turn right, walk around the church into Kerkplein, then turn left into Oude Molenstraat, one of the oldest streets in the city; its houses have been extensively restored by The Hague Urban Renewal Organization. Behind 18th- and 19th-century façades, many of the buildings here date from the 16th century or even earlier, especially those on the even-numbered (east) side. At nos. 23–27 a family coat-of-arms of the founder, Jacob Frederik van Beieren van Schagen, marks a former almshouse for the old men of the city, endowed in 1773. Opposite, at no. 32, is a typical wealthy patrician's home, with an ornate Louis XIV façade which was added in 1747 to a 16th-century townhouse.

At the corner of Juffrouw Idastraat, detour briefly left along that street to visit the Old Catholic Church, built in 1722 and, in accordance with the Protestant mood of the time, discreetly hidden between the houses of the Idastraat and the Molenstraat (enter by Juffrouw Idastraat no. 7). The church is lavishly decorated in the style of Louis XIV, with fine furnishings and elegantly carved high altarpiece, pulpit and communion rail. Compared with the austere interiors of the Dutch Protestant churches, the effect is almost overwhelming.

Retrace your steps to the Oude Molenstraat, turn left, then go right, along Molenstraat. At the end, turn left into Noordeinde, one of The Hague's smartest shopping streets, with a number of expensive antique dealers. At the corner of Heulstraat, pass the dull 19th-century Waalsekerk (Walloon Church) and walk to the Noordeinde Palace, at Noordeinde no. 68. This is one of the highlights of this walk.

In 1591 the States of Holland provided a house here for Louise de Coligny, the widowed fourth wife of William I of Orange, and her children. In the early 17th century the house was extended and given as a palace to Stadhouder Frederick Henry, William's grandson, and his mother. Frederick Henry had it extensively refurbished in 1640, and until the French Occupation of the Napoleonic period it continued to be a residence of the Stadhouder. It was further restored and extended in 1813 after the crowning of William I as King of the Netherlands, and underwent yet another restoration in the 1970s. It is now used by Queen Beatrix for royal and diplomatic receptions.

The Noordeinde wing is a fine example of mid-17th-century Classical Baroque. Decorative railings connect the two side-wings, and in front of them stands a mounted statue of Prince William of Orange. Elected Stadhouder after expelling the Spaniards, he is the great-grandfather of William III, who became King of England and Scotland in 1688 through his marriage to Mary Stuart and the deposition of King James II and VII. Confusingly, William III is generally known in Britain as William of Orange.

From Noordeinde, bear right up Paleisstraat to no. 3, the Gothic Hall, built in 1842 during the reign of King William II. Educated at Oxford, William II was a great fan of English Gothic, and he endowed The Hague with a number of public buildings in this style. This is one of the finest, with a beautiful wooden roof and a fine organ by J. Batz. If you're here on a Wednesday, you'll find the stalls of The Hague's regular stamp market laid out around the horse-chestnut tree in the square between the hall and the Noordeinde Palace. Next door, at no. 3 Paleisstraat, you discover the Dutch Games of Chance Museum, in the Dutch State Lottery Association building. It displays lottery equipment and life-size tableaux of games of chance through history, including a model of an early lottery, held in Leiden in 1596.

At the end of Paleisstraat, turn right into Oranjestraat. Your next landmark is the spire of the neo-Gothic St Jacobus Church, another work by the prolific P.J.H. Cuypers. The triumphant spire soars more than 90m (273ft) skyward, and the finely preserved interior is cluttered with numerous altars, statues and stained-glass windows. It is one of three Catholic churches built in the city after the Netherlands had once again begun to permit open Catholic worship and the re-establishment of the Church hierarchy.

Reaching Parkstraat, turn right, then at its end turn left into Lange Voorhout. On the corner, at Lange Voorhout no. 2, is the Monastery Church, built around 1400. Its Dominican monks were ousted during the Reformation, and it became an artillery foundry. It is now used by the city's Reformed Duinoord congregation; an Apostle Window by Lou Asperslagh and a mosaic of the Last Supper came from an earlier Duinoord church, demolished in 1842. A little further up Lange Voorhout, on your left, is the 17th-century Pages' House, with one of the few surviving step-gables in the city. Built in 1618, it was originally used by the master-founder of the cannon foundry in the Monastery Church. Later, the pages of the royal court lived here, and since 1867 it has been used by the Red Cross organization.

An elegant avenue

Turn right at the corner with Klein Kazernestraat, cross Hoge Nieuwstraat, and turn left into Lange Vijverberg. Built on the sand that had been dredged out in the 14th century to create the decorative Hofvijver Lake, on your right, this avenue is lined with fine 18th-century buildings which look across to the front of the Binnenhof and the Upper House.

At no. 14, the Museum Bredius has a fine collection of works by Rembrandt, Albert Cuyp (1620–1691), Aert van der Neer (*c.*1603–1677) and a number of minor painters, hung in a fine Rococo interior dating from 1756. From the museum, walk to the corner of Toernooiveld (Tournament Field). As the name of this street implies, in medieval times it was used for knightly jousts. Just before you reach it, close to the corner of Korte Vijverberg at Korte Vijverberg no. 7, you find the Historic Museum of The Hague. This is housed in a 17th-century building with elegant Ionic pilasters that was built for the bowmen of the Company of St Sebastian. It is a new museum (opened in 1986), and well worth a look if you want to know more about how The Hague has grown up over the centuries.

A little further on, at Toernooiveld no. 5, a plaque set in the 18th-century frame-gable depicts St Joris (St George) and the dragon, and bears the date 1625. This was the guildhouse of the Crossbowmen of St George. The pretty octagonal turret which juts out on the right-hand side of the building is a later addition.

Now cross the street, turn left, and walk one block back along Voorhout to Lange Voorhout, crossing it and turning left to glance at the frontage of the Royal Library at nos. 32–36. Completed in 1736 and expanded in 1760, this was the home of one Adrienne Marguerite Huguetan and is one of the finest examples of an aristocratic residence in the Louis XIV style.

Retrace your steps a short distance, then carry on to the city's finest hostelry, the Hotel des Indes, a witty, eclectic building planned as the town residence of Baron van Brienen. It has been an elegant hotel since the 1880s. If you can afford it, this is the place to stay on a visit to The Hague; its guests have included Paul Kruger, Winston Churchill, Haile Selassie, Charles Lindbergh and Anna Pavlova, who died of pneumonia here. The heating is better these days.

Bear right, across the northern end of Lange Voorhout, to the Lange Voorhout Palace at no. 74. The building dates from 1764, when it was the residence of Anthony Patras, the Friesland delegate to the States-General. A royal residence from 1845, it is now a museum which offers a changing programme of art and historic exhibitions. The interior has some fine Rococo detail, and the façade is a good example of the transition between Louis XV and Louis XVI styles. Napoleon spent a night here in 1811.

Walk past the palace to the corner of Lange Voorhout and cross Korte Voorhout. Facing you, close to the corner of Schouwburgstraat, is an elegant building with a refined arched façade in early Louis XVI style. This is the Royal Theatre, originally commissioned in 1766 as a large city palace for Carel van Nassau-Weilburg, daughter of Prince William IV.

From the Royal Theatre, turn right and walk along Schouwburgstraat and Bleijenburgstraat to Herengracht, and retrace your initial steps back to the station.

The Hague 2: Art, antiques and parks

The Hague has some of Europe's finest antiquarian shops and auction rooms. During the Dutch colonial era, its close links with the Far East made it a centre for exotic art, antiques and curiosities from all over Asia and the world. This long walk takes you through quaint streets packed with shops, galleries and markets selling everything under the sun. Real enthusiasts should time their visit for late August, when The Hague Tourist Office (VVV) organizes special Art and Antique Days with the backing of antiques dealers, art galleries and auction houses. It is also worth asking VVV for the 'The Hague Chequebook' — consisting of discount vouchers for museums, attractions, restaurants and shops — and for the monthly Haags Werk brochure issued by Stroom, The Hague's visual-arts centre, which tells you who is exhibiting and where. This walk includes also several fascinating museums and the famous miniature village of Madurodam, set in the huge green space of the Scheveningse Bosjes.

Start:	Den Haag Hollands Spoor Station; trams 8, 9, 11, 12; trains to and from Amsterdam Centraal Station go 4–6 times hourly and take about 45 minutes
Finish:	Madurodam; take tram 1 or 9 to return to Hollands Spoor Station for trains to Amsterdam
Length:	8km (5 miles)
Time:	All day, with shopping and museum visits
Refreshments:	Many bars and restaurants in Korte Poten and Denneweg, cafés in museums; grand cafés in the Lange Houtstraat
Which day:	Not Sunday or Monday, unless the Voorhout Market has top priority for you
To visit:	● Voorhout Antique and Book Market: mid-May to beginning of October, Thursday 10.00–19.00 and Sunday 11.00–17.00
	● Panorama Mesdag: Monday–Saturday 10.00–17.00, Sunday 12.00–17.00
	● Mesdag Museum: Tuesday–Saturday 10.00–17.00, Sunday 13.00–17.00
	● Vredespaleis (Peace Palace): Monday–Friday 10.00–15.00, tours hourly except 13.00
	● Omniversum: hourly programmes Tuesday–Thursday 11.00–16.00, Friday–Sunday 11.00–21.00
	● Gemeentemuseum: Tuesday–Sunday 11.00–17.00
	● Museo: Tuesday–Friday 10.00–1700, Weekends 12.00–17.00
	● Madurodam: March 23–June 30 09.00–20.00; July–August 09.00–22.00; September–March 09.00–1700

Starting from the Hollands Spoor Station, turn left onto the Spui and walk up to its junction with Herengracht, where you turn right. Herengracht takes a kink to the left, then to the right where it joins Korte Poten. A detour along Herengracht takes you to the decorative canal bridge which leads across to the Koningskade. In 1882 Vincent Van Gogh painted this corner of Prinsengracht and Herengracht from the viewpoint of the lawn behind the bridge. On the other side, a group of statuary depicts the digging of The Hague's ring of canals, begun on the advice of Prince Maurice of Nassau, the second Stadhouder, around 1613. A motto below reads 'Door Burgers daad, op Maurits raad, deez cingel onstaat' ('By citizens' deed, on Maurice's counsel, this canal is built'). The Hague never received a city charter and so did not have the right to build a city wall; the Prinsengracht canal ring served as protection instead. Further down Herengracht, the pretty, highly decorated building at no. 19 was once the home of the Princess of Orange, Maurice's sister.

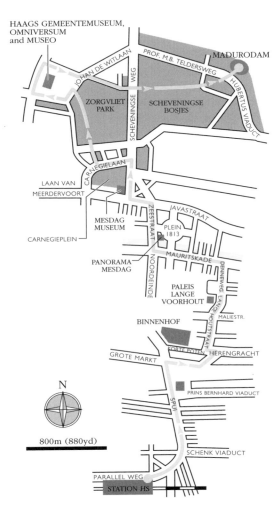

Take a U-turn back to the Korte Poten, a short esplanade leading to the Plein, The Hague's main square. In the centre of the square stands a statue of William of Orange, erected in 1848. It was one of the first grand statues in The Hague, and caused a scandal at its unveiling. For some reason, the dog at William's feet was considered inappropriate; the story goes, innocuously enough, that the loyal pet's barking alerted the prince to an enemy raid during the wars with Spain, thereby saving his life.

Turn right and walk along Lange Houtstraat. On a Thursday or a Sunday, detour left into Lange Voorhout for a rummage around the open-air antiques and book market. Lined with centuries-old lime trees and gracious 18th-century buildings, with the decorative Hof Vijver Lake and the façade of the Binnenhof on your left, this is sometimes claimed to be the most beautiful avenue in the whole of Europe. Expert antiquarians may be able to find valuable first editions among the dusty leather-bound volumes, but you can also shop for hand-made jewellery, posters, prints and paintings.

Retrace your steps (if you have taken this detour) to the corner of Toernooiveld and Denneweg and turn left into Denneweg.

A street of antiques

This splendid street has a charmingly raffish style and is an antique-browser's heaven, with dozens of shops on the main street and in its narrow side-lanes. A short detour right, into Maliestraat, takes you to the little bridge over Smidswater. It is The Hague's prettiest canal prospect.

Mata Hari (1876–1917), the epitome of the beautiful, femme fatale spy, lived here at no. 16 before leaving in 1905 for France and a career as a dancer and, it is claimed, a double agent. Born Margarete Gertrude Zelle in Leeuwarden, she adopted a glamorous but completely fake Oriental identity and had many lovers in high government and military circles on both the German and French sides during World War I. In 1917 a French court-martial convicted her of spying for the Germans and she was executed.

Drop into Cachot Antiek at no. 18 for antiques and curios, Takayama at no. 18 for oriental prints and paintings, Bodes & Bode at no. 50 for antique jewellery and silverware, and the Haagsche Kunstkring at no. 64 for works of art.

Halfway down Denneweg, turn into Spekstraat, where you will find antiquarian books and drawings at Imagerie, at no. 2, and two more galleries, Roger at no. 3 and Spektakel at no. 5A.

The road to Scheveningen

Denneweg itself is one of the old roads leading from The Hague to its seaside suburb, Scheveningen. It may have been a Roman road in antiquity. It is an almost solid expanse of antiques shops and art galleries, with twenty or more jostling for attention in one short block.

At the end of the Denneweg, turn left into the Mauritskade and left again, keeping the canal on your right. Named after Prince Maurice of Nassau, the canal originally formed part of the city's defences; it was not until the 19th century that The Hague expanded beyond this boundary into what until then had been pasture and farmland. Most of the houses along the canal quay date from the 19th century; a plaque at no. 43 marks the birthplace of the noted Dutch author Louis Couperus (1863–1923).

At the junction with Noordeinde, turn right, cross the canal and walk along Zeestraat to the Panorama Mesdag at no. 65B. Within is one of the largest paintings in the world. It was painted in 1881 by Hendrik Willem Mesdag (1831–1915), his wife and some friends. Standing on a low platform, you find yourself surrounded by an extraordinary circular canvas 15m (45ft) tall and some 112m (400ft) around. Mesdag and his colleagues of the Hague School specialized in seascapes; the panorama depicts sand dunes, seaside, walkers and their dogs, driftwood, empty bottles and the Scheveningen skyline. A detachment of cavalry, exercising their horses on the sands, adds movement to the composition; gulls fly overhead and fishermen mend their nets beside dinghies drawn up along the tideline. All the scene needs to become a perfect imitation of the real thing is the cry of gulls and a faint smell of fish. It took the painters four months to complete this extraordinary work.

Walk on along Zeestraat and turn left onto Laan Van Meerdervoort for one block, then cross the avenue. At no. 7F is the Mesdag Museum, which has a wider selection of the works of this painter as well as works by his contemporaries. Mesdag commissioned the building to house his paintings, and left it to the Dutch nation on his death. As well as the seascapes favoured by the Hague School, it contains paintings by French artists of the Barbizon school, including Jean François Millet (1814–1875) and Jean Corot (1796–1875).

Turn left out of the museum and walk along Carnegielaan towards the Carnegieplein and the eclectic Vredespaleis (Peace Palace) building, which houses the International Court of Justice, better known as the World Court.

Set up in 1899 by the Hague Peace Conference, the court theoretically has global jurisdiction and is widely respected for its neutrality, though some governments – notably that of the USA – continue to flout its judgements when it suits them. The Peace Palace was begun in 1903 with a $1.5 million donation from the Scots–American millionaire Andrew Carnegie, and incorporates decorative and functional elements donated by many nations.

Leaving the Carnegieplein, turn left and walk along the semicircular Carnegielaan. Crossing the long, thin decorative lake, turn right and walk through the green space of the Zorgvliet Park. After about 800m (half a mile) you emerge at the junction of two major avenues, President Kennedylaan and Johan de Witlaan. On the opposite side of the avenue is a complex of three museums.

The order in which you visit these will depend on when you arrive. The Omniversum, a high-tech planetarium-style attraction, operates a changing schedule of pop-science shows with lasers, video and all-around sound hourly on the hour. The Haags Gemeentemuseum (Hague Municipal Museum), next door at Stadhouderslaan no. 41 is another work by H.P. Berlage, architect of the Amsterdam Stock Exchange (see page 20) and other major buildings in Amsterdam and The Hague. The interior is clinically clean and bright, with modern Dutch artists including the COBRA (Copenhagen, Brussels, Amsterdam) painters hung beside earlier 20th-century masters, including Mondrian, Picasso, Schiele, Monet and the Impressionists of the Hague School. There is a also a fine collection of crystal and silver, plus a huge assortment of musical instruments. Sharing the Stadhouderslaan no. 41 complex is the Museo, a high-tech science museum with lots of hands-on exhibits.

The Netherlands in miniature

Now go back across Johan de Witlaan into the Zorgvliet. Cross the park and the Scheveningseweg to find yourself in a huge green expanse of landscaped woods and lawns, the Scheveningse Bosjes. Angle through the park to reach Prof. M.B. Teldersweg, just before it enters the Hubertus Viaduct traffic system; cross the avenue and, at no. 175 Haringkade, enter Holland in miniature.

Madurodam is really for children, but most grown-ups find it hard to resist taking a step back into childhood when confronted with this scale-model Dutch town, whose red-tiled houses come barely to knee-height. Even the cathedral bell-tower is only about 5m (16ft) tall. Madurodam is a conglomeration of 1:25 scale models of buildings and monuments from all over the Netherlands, complete with tiny toy people, cars, cows and windmills to lend verisimilitude. Here a crowd of tiny tourists are gathered outside a dolls'-house-sized model of the Royal Palace. There a Lilliputian sunbather lies on a rooftop sunbed. After sunset, the miniature streets are lit by more than 50,000 bulbs. It is the ultimate Toytown. You may recognize some of the streets and buildings featured in this book, and there are even models of Rotterdam's giant Europoort and Amsterdam's Schiphol Airport. During the summer months, a sound and light show picks out Madurodam's tiny streets.

Stay here as long as you want to, then take tram 1 or 9 to return to Hollands Spoor Station for trains to Amsterdam.

Scheveningen

About 3km (two miles) northwest of The Hague lies the North Sea beach resort and fishing harbour of Scheveningen, now virtually a suburb of The Hague. This walk shows you two faces of Scheveningen – the surviving traditional fishing village and the modern beach resort.

Start/finish: Keizerstraat; trams 1, 9 from Hollands Spoor Station, which is served by trains to and from Amsterdam
Length: 5km (3½ miles)
Time: 2½hr
Refreshments: Bars and restaurants on Keizerstraat and along the beachfront; Scheveningen is known for its excellent seafood restaurants
Which day: Any day
To visit:
- Vlissingen Zee Museum (Sea Museum): Monday–Saturday 10.00–17.00, Sunday 13.00–17.00
- Scheveningen Museum: April–October Monday–Saturday 10.00–17.00, November–March Tuesday–Saturday 10.00–17.00
- Scheveningen Sea-Life Centre: daily 10.00–18.00, July–August 10.00–20.00

You start the walk where Keizerstraat, the fashionable main street which runs at right angles to the seafront, becomes Prins Willemstraat. This street is an extension of Scheveningseweg, the long avenue connecting the beach resort of Scheveningen with The Hague.

Scheveningen makes its first appearance in the records of the counts of Holland around the year 1280. An earlier village had apparently been buried by the shifting sand dunes on which it was built. Until the 19th century it remained a tiny settlement, with some two to three hundred homes and about 3500 fisherfolk making a bare living from the sea. The village remained vulnerable to flood and storm; the Great Flood (Allerheiligenvloed) of 1570 swept away every house between the Oude Kerk and the beach.

The first holidaymakers

As early as the 17th century, the burghers of The Hague began to build seaside homes here, enjoying the fresh air away from the smoke and the smelly canals of the city. The real boom came in the 19th century, when sea bathing became fashionable all over Europe. In 1818 Jacob Pronk opened the first Scheveningen Bathing House, and other fashionable establishments followed: the Grand Hotel, the Hotel des Galeries, the Palace Hotel and others. Sadly, none of them survived World War II

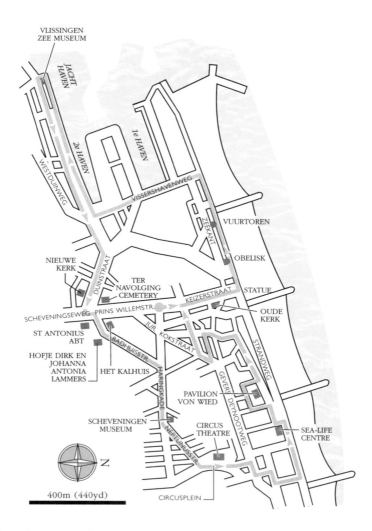

VLISSINGEN
ZEE MUSEUM

JACHT
HAVEN

2e HAVEN

1e HAVEN

WESTDUINWEG

VISSERSHAVENWEG

ZEEKANT

VUURTOREN

NIEUWE
KERK

DUINSTRAAT

OBELISK

TER
NAVOLGING
CEMETERY

KEIZERSTRAAT

STATUE

SCHEVENINGSEWEG PRINS WILLEMSTR.

TUR

OUDE
KERK

ST ANTONIUS
ABT

BADHUISSTR

KOKSTRAAT

STRANDWEG

HOFJE DIRK EN
JOHANNA
ANTONIA
LAMMERS

HET KALHUIS

HARINGKADE

GEVERS DEYNOOTWEG

PAVILION
VON WIED

SCHEVENINGEN
MUSEUM

NEPTUNUSSTR.

CIRCUS
THEATRE

SEA-LIFE
CENTRE

N

400m (440yd)

CIRCUSPLEIN

and the urban renewal which followed; only the fabulous Kurhaus (see page 98) survives as a reminder of Scheveningen's grand Victorian heyday.

The Keizerstraat has been Scheveningen's main street since the earliest times, and many of its older buildings are worth a closer look. Before walking towards the beach, note the tiny tower, with its winged griffins, at nos. 327–329. Erected in 1900, this building was the dairy of the royal household, as you can partly infer from the carvings of dairy cattle, milk churns and cheese- and butter-making utensils above the door.

A little further down, at nos. 215–215A, with a striking Jugendstil façade, is the prettiest building on the Keizerstraat. Built in 1903, this Jugendstil apartment building blends 19th- and 20th-century styles.

At no. 58, the front of an 18th-century building incorporates a stone commemorating the landing of Prince William of Orange (later King William I) at Scheveningen on 30 November 1813, an event that signalled the end of the period of French dominance in the Netherlands. The building was once the parsonage of the Old Reformed Church.

Another and much older church awaits you at no. 8 Keizerstraat. The Oude Kerk was built around 1500, and stands on the foundations of an older church building, which was destroyed in the great storm of 1470. The Gothic building passed into the hands of the Dutch Reformed Church following the Reformation. Between 1957 and 1959 it was restored, with the addition of a vestry. Among its odder treasures are the jawbone and vertebrae of a sperm whale which was stranded at Scheveningen in 1617. The carved pulpit dates from 1756, the organ from 1765 and the oldest choir-stall from 1662.

Along the shore

Walk around the church to face the North Sea. A bronze statue on a low rise overlooking the beach is your next landmark. Unveiled by Queen Beatrix in 1982, the statue is of a fisherwoman in traditional costume, gazing out to sea. It is a memorial to all the fisherfolk of Scheveningen who have lost their lives at sea. A few hundred older women still wear the traditional costume of Scheveningen's fisher community when going to church and on special occasions: long black skirts and jackets and immaculate white cotton caps held in place by elaborate, solid-gold hatpins, which are treasured family heirlooms.

˙ From the statue, turn left and, keeping the sea on your right, walk towards the stone obelisk you can see a short way along Zeekant, the beach esplanade. Erected in 1865 in memory of the triumphant return of William of Orange in 1813, it celebrates another of the country's victories over foreign domination.

Walk on along the esplanade towards the Vuurtoren (lighthouse) at no. 13 Zeekant. Built in 1875, the ten-storey, 36m (120ft) lighthouse is a national monument. In clear weather its light can be seen up to 40km (25 miles) out to sea. Scheveningen has had a lighthouse since the earliest days. In 1589 the wooden light-tower burned down – the lighthouses of those times, being fuelled by wood or coal, were always at risk from fire. The existing tower – one of a chain of 14 along the Dutch coast – was originally lit by gas, but its powerful lamp now runs on electricity.

Walk on along the seafront to the flight of steps at the end of the sea wall, and descend the steps to the Vissershavenweg. Turn your back to the sea and return towards the harbour. The early-morning fish auction, once one of the sights of Scheveningen, is now conducted by computer and sadly no longer open to visitors.

Thanks to the dwindling of the North Sea fishing industry, it is hard to imagine what the Scheveniningen quayside must have been like in its bustling heyday. Curiously, until the late 19th century the town had no harbour at all. Fishermen used flat-bottomed boats, called bomschuiten, which could be hauled safely up the beach out of reach of the waves. The faster, deeper-hulled luggers which came into use in the 1850s, however, needed the shelter of a proper harbour. By 1858, plans were complete but there was endless debate over the 1.5 million guilders needed to finance the dredging and construction of the quays. The municipality really dragged its feet – for almost 40 years! Then, just before Christmas 1894, a fierce gale wreaked havoc on the unprotected fleet of 150 bomschuiten drawn up on the beach, a disaster immortalized by Hendrik Willem Mesdag (see page 91) in his painting *Storm 1894*. More than twenty were completely wrecked, and half the fleet was severely damaged. The initial new harbour was finally opened in 1904, but the opening ceremony was marred when the first ship to enter ran aground and was wrecked. It soon became clear that the new harbour was too small to shelter all the fleet, and did not offer full protection from rough seas. A second harbour was opened in 1931, and this ushered in an era of prosperity for the fishing community. The third harbour, built in the 1970s, is nowadays used by Dutch/UK cargo vessels; a fourth harbour, for freight vessels, is planned.

Around the harbour

Keeping the harbour to your right, follow Vissershavenweg along to Tweede Haven (Second Harbour), then turn right and walk along the quay to its end, where the Vlissingen Sea Museum, at Dr Lelykade no. 39, overlooks the inner Jacht Haven. The museum features exhibits of more than 25,000 shells, corals and starfish from all over the world; a 'Diorama of the Abyss' displays images of weird luminous creatures and needle-jawed fish from the pitch-dark depths of the oceans.

From here, double back along the quay to the inner end of Tweede Haven, then walk along Westduinweg and turn right onto Duinstraat. On your right, at the far end of the street, is the Nieuwe Kerk (New Church), built in 1893 to accommodate Scheveningen's expanding population. The façade shows characteristic Dutch Renaissance influences.

Opposite the Nieuwe Kerk is the Ter Navolging Cemetery; the coat-of-arms of Baron Pieter Anthony of Huybert, from which the Scheveningen city coat-of-arms derives, is displayed on the cemetery's left outer wall. Among the numerous graves within are those of the 18th-century writers Betje Wolff (1738–1804) and Aagje Deken (1741–1804) and the 19th-century conservative politician Groen van Prinsterer (1801–1876).

At the end of Duinstraat, cross the Scheveningseweg. Detour briefly to your right to visit the Roman Catholic Church of St Antonius Abt at Scheveningseweweg no. 235, designed by J. and P. Cuypers in 1925 and the only church in the Netherlands with an Art Deco interior. The mosaics that adorn it are by Anton Molkenboer and depict women in traditional costumes of the 19th century.

Scheveningseweg, the first paved road in the Netherlands, was built in 1666 in response to campaigning by Constantijn Huygens (1596–1687), the poet who was also personal secretary to the Prince of Orange. Traders and travellers had to pay a toll to use the road; this was abolished in 1889, by which time anyway other roads provided toll-free alternatives. In the Scheveningen Museum you can see a model of the old tollgate.

Walk back to the junction of Scheveningseweg and Badhuisstraat and turn right. Badhuisstraat is an unspectacular modern shopping street with a handful of interesting buildings. Het Kalhuis, at Badhuisstraat no. 177, now a community centre, was built in 1900 as the town's new post office and has an unusual, richly decorated brick façade and chimney. Almost opposite, on your right-hand side, at nos. 170–188, is a beautifully restored almshouse-courtyard, Hofje Dirk en Johanna Antonia Lammers. This was built in 1875 by a benevolent society to house Scheveningen's widows and spinsters, as it still does. In the middle of the pretty courtyard is an antique water-pump.

Further down Badhuisstraat, at no. 114, is a mural painting, *De Fraanse Poort*, done by Kees van der Vlies. It depicts a day in the life of a Scheveningen fisher family.

Badhuisstraat leads you to Marcelisstraat. Follow this street until you reach the Haringkade.

The Haringkade (Herring Quay) was an inland dockside. Deeper-hulled herring-boats, unable to land at Scheveningen until the harbour was opened at the beginning of the 20th century, had to unload their catch at nearby Vlaardingen or Maassluis. The fish were then transported to Scheveningen by canal, and unloaded at this quay. Dug in 1860, the canal was supposed to open to the sea, but was never completed; the villagers feared that breaching the protective wall of dunes would make Scheveningen even more vulnerable to floods, and in due course the opening of the new harbour made the canal redundant. It was finally filled in in 1971.

Cross Haringkade into Neptunusstraat and walk to the junction with Stevinstraat, where Neptunusstraat forks to your left; follow it. On the left side of the street, at no. 92, is the Scheveningen Museum, landmarked by a beacon from one of the old seafront jetties. There are tableaux of fisherfolk and craftsmen at work, models of boats, maps, instruments, paintings and prints, all relating to Scheveningen's history as a fishing community and as a seaside resort.

Once you have prowled around the museum, come out of it, turn left, walk down Neptunusstraat, and turn left again. On your left, at Circusstraat no. 4, is a dramatic domed building with a fantastic arched portico and with huge portholes piercing its two-storey façade. This is the Circus Theatre. Built in 1904 as a permanent venue for the splendid circuses that were popular with holidaymakers in Scheveningen, the building attracted Europe's greatest circus performers. In the early 1960s, now that circuses had become no longer popular, it closed, reopening as an arts centre in 1964. Presently owned by Joop van den Ende Productions, it was renovated in 1993 and is now used for top international musicals and revues.

A grand survivor

From the Circusplein, walk towards the sea and turn right on Gevers Deynootweg, then left on Gevers Deynootplein, a square dominated by the imposing domes and turrets of the grand Steigenberger Kurhaus Hotel, into which you can take a quick exploratory detour.

Built between 1884 and 1887, the hotel is one of the last survivors of Scheveningen's Golden Age as a 19th-century resort for the aristocracy and the crowned heads of Europe. The hotel got off to a poor start when it burned to the ground on 1 September 1886, little more than a year after it had first been opened. The fire is said to have been caused by one of the maids of the wealthy Heineken brewing family, who were staying at the hotel; upsetting a spirit burner, she set alight a curtain and the flames quickly spread. Undeterred, the owners rebuilt the hotel, which reopened in June the following year and has been run in the grand-hotel tradition ever since. Guests have included Winston Churchill, Marlene Dietrich and Luciano Pavarotti. The lobby area is truly palatial, with splendid giltwork and ceiling paintings ornamenting the interior of the vast dome.

The pier

Leaving the hotel, walk around to the seaward side and come onto Strandweg, Scheveningen's seafront boulevard. Looking out to sea, you see on your right the Scheveningen Pier, stretching more than 380m (415yd) out to sea. The first promenade pier was built in 1901 and survived until World War II, when it was damaged by fire and then demolished by the German occupying forces, who feared it might be used in an Allied landing. A new pier was built in 1961, and became one of the resort's most popular attractions. By the 1990s, however, it had fallen into disrepair. The new owners, the Van der Valk property company, have redeveloped it and have already reopened three restaurants on the pier, including a huge dining-room – with seating for 1000 – in the rotunda at the seaward end.

Go left along the boulevard and past the front of the Kurhaus to the next block and the Scheveningen Sea-Life Centre, at Strandweg no. 13. This was originally an indoor tropical wave pool; now sharks, skates and stingrays have taken the place of swimmers. A transparent underwater tunnel takes you right in among them

Leave the boulevard by the steps behind the Sea-Life Centre and come to Scheveningsesalg. Cross the street, and take another flight of steps to Harteveltstraat, then turn immediately right down Pellenaerstraat. The Pavilion von Wied is 100m (110yd) in front of you.

A sleepless queen

This pavilion, with its Neoclassical pillared portico, was ordered by King William I in 1826 as a gift to his queen, Frederica Louise Wilhelmina van Pruissen. Frederica was an insomniac, and William hoped the sea air and the soothing sound of the waves would help cure her. The building was little-used in the decades following her death, in 1837, and in 1918 it passed into the hands of the De Witte Literary Society. The entrance-way is now decorated with charming mural paintings.

At the end of Pellenaerstraat, turn right into Jongeneelstraat. The steps at the end of this street lead you back to the sea; turn left, keeping the beach on your right. This stretch of shore is known as Seinpostduin (Signpost Dune); in Napoleon's time a wooden semaphore post stood here, one of a sequence of hundreds that stretched from the Netherlands all the way to Paris, so that messages could be rushed to the Emperor. Hendrik Willem Mesdag used this dune as his vantage-point for the sketches he did for his famous panorama of Scheveningen and The Hague, *The Mesdag Panorama* (see page 91).

Turning your back to the sea, walk up Zeeweg and Zeestraat, cross Wassenaarse-straat, and walk along Zeilstraat. This part of town is one of the last surviving pockets of old Scheveningen. Typical fishermen's cottages, with their characteristic coloured wooden shutters, are now much in demand by trendy purchasers. Take some time to wander at random through what was the heart of the original fishing village before you return to the Keizerstraat and the end of this walk.

Rotterdam 1: Weena to the Maas

*Amsterdam can sometimes seem a little like a living museum; by contrast,
Rotterdam, though it has been an important seaport for over two centuries, is one of
Europe's newest cities.*
*Virtually levelled by the bombing of both sides during World War II, Rotterdam
has been rebuilt during the past half-century according to a grand design, to which the
finishing touches are now being put. The city boasts an exciting concentration of
modern European architecture, including dynamic public buildings, offices, private
homes and apartment complexes. As in other Dutch cities, many people still live
right in the city-centre, humanizing what might otherwise be a visually stunning
but rather sterile environment. Rotterdam is also proud of its collection of public art:
monuments, statues and modernistic sculpture adorn its street corners, squares and
parks. The difference from central Amsterdam's tidy, dolls'-house-like 17th- and
18th-century streets and canal-sides could not be greater, and, whereas Amsterdam
seems to turn its back firmly on the sea, Rotterdam makes the 500m (550yd) wide
River Maas one of its central features. The Maas is always busy with shipping
heading to and from the North Sea and the waterfront of the vast Europoort
complex downriver, 48km (30 miles) long; hundreds of cranes can be seen bristling on
the western skyline. Downtown Rotterdam looks across the Nieuwe Maas to docklands
on the south bank, an area that has become a focus for urban regeneration, with
the opening, scheduled for 1996, of a giant suspension bridge linking the two
halves of the city.*
*The first of our two Rotterdam walks takes you through the city's modernistic downtown
to its historic waterfront, taking in a cross-section of 20th-century architecture.*

Start:	Metro Stationsplein/Rotterdam Centraal Station/Centraal Bus Station; intercity trains from Amsterdam and The Hague; all buses
Finish:	Metro Churchillsplein; buses 32, 49; trams 3, 6, 7
Length:	3km (2 miles)
Time:	1–2hr
Refreshments:	Lots of trendy open-air café-restaurants around the Oude Haven
Which day:	Any day
To visit:	• St Laurens Kerk (Grote Kerk): Tuesday–Saturday 10.00–16.00; tower open third Saturday of each month during May–September
	• Grotekerkplein Stamp, Coin and Book Market: Tuesday and Saturday 09.30–16.00
	• Grote Markt: weekday and Saturday mornings
	• Openlucht Binnenvaart Museum (Open-Air Inland Navigation Museum): daily during daylight hours

● Mariniers Museum der Koninklijke Marine (Royal Marine
   Corps Museum): Tuesday–Saturday 10.00–17.00, Sunday
   11.00–17.00

Stationsplein's east side is dominated by the multi-storey mirrored façades of two giant office blocks, setting the architectural tone for the downtown area. From the southeast corner of the square, turn east onto Weena, the city's business heart, a corridor of space-age buildings whose gleaming walls mirror each other seemingly to infinity. Walk east to the circular Hofplein, which you can recognize by the curtains of spray tumbling from its central fountain; cross the circle and continue on the south side of Pompenburg for about 50m (55yd) to come to the skeletal columns and portico of the Nieuw Delfs Poort (New Delft Gate), the latest of the city's many exciting pieces of public art. An imaginative interpretation of the gateway which originally pierced the old city walls here, this pavilion-like building houses the Classical-style stone reliefs of lions and mythical heroes which adorned the original 18th-century gateway, demolished by bombing during World War II.

Turn to your right and cross to Doelstraat, which is conveniently landmarked by what must be Europe's prettiest police headquarters, a Cubist building completely covered in Art Deco turquoise tiles. It occupies the entire northeast side of the street. In the middle of Doelstraat, which is a pedestrian street, stand a two-storey-high black rectangular marble gateway and a tall bronze column.

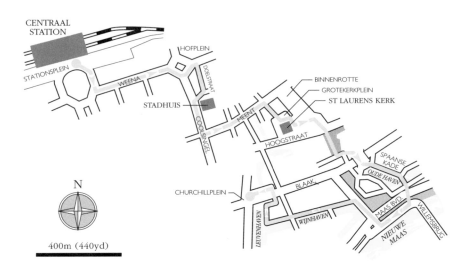

Monument to commerce

Continue down Doelstraat to reach the back of the Stadhuis, an imposing grey sandstone building capped by a green bronze clock tower, and turn right onto Doelwater. Follow this small side-street for a further 75m (83yd) to join Coolsingel, the main traffic artery of central Rotterdam. Turn left onto Coolsingel's east side for a look at the Stadhuis's façade and statuary.

Begun in 1914, the building was completed in 1920 and is a suitably impressive monument to Rotterdam's commercial empire. Graceful stone Muses, each pair surmounted by a Latin motto, flank the balconied second-storey windows at each corner. At the north end of the frontage sits a statue of the scholar and jurist Hugo Grotius (1583–1645). Born in Delft, Grotius – as was then usual among men of letters – Latinized his name from its Dutch form, Huig de Groot. The father of modern international law, which he outlined in his treatise De Jure Pacis et Belli (Of the Law of Peace and War), Grotius saw the horrors of the religious wars which racked Europe during his lifetime and was moved by them to create the first code of conduct for nations at war. His work prefigures the conditions of the Geneva Convention. His outspoken beliefs, both religious and political, led to his being first imprisoned, then driven into exile in France.

At the south end of the Stadhuis front stands a bronze statue of Johan (Jan) van Oldenbarnevelt, Pensioner of Rotterdam 1576–1586 and States Advocate 1586–1619. A line of reliefs set in the arches above the Stadhuis's second-floor windows commemorate other great lawgivers: clearly Rotterdam's city fathers felt that their own great men, such as the theologian Erasmus and the jurists and statesmen J. van der Veken and P. de Hoogh (1629–1684), ranked with ancient figures like Solomon and Pericles.

Erasmus of Rotterdam (1467–1536) was a moderate Catholic reformer and scholar whose work helped pave the way for more radical thinkers like Martin Luther and John Calvin. Influenced by the ancient Greek and Roman philosophers, he wrote a lifetime's worth of polemics against pedantry, superstition and corruption within the Church, and for a time (1500–1513) was Professor of Divinity at Cambridge University. In particular, his determination to make the Bible accessible to ordinary folk by translating it from Latin into everyday language was revolutionary. He believed that the Roman Catholic Church could be reformed from within, and was disappointed by the violence and intolerance which quickly became part of the Reformation he helped to begin.

Alternating with these stern faces are plaques symbolizing trade, art, science and law. Above these, on the higher gables, are the coats-of-arms of South Holland (a red lion rampant on a gold field), the Netherlands (a gold lion, armed and rampant on a blue field) and the six prominent families of the city.

Just south of the Stadhuis stands Rotterdam's old Central Post Office, a massive and not wildly prepossessing piece of 1920s Futurist architecture made more interesting by the decorative frieze of ships, semi-mythical creatures and stylized figures celebrating the Dutch overseas empire. South of the Post Office, turn left onto Meentstraat, crossing one of Rotterdam's few canals; unlike those of Amsterdam it is lined not with tall medieval houses but with modern apartment complexes. In spring the canal's murky waters attract great-crested grebes, which lay their eggs aboard island nests haphazardly built of reeds and scraps of litter.

Go south along Coolsingel and turn left along Meent. Down the third street off Meent to your right you will see the clock tower of the St Laurens Kerk (Church of St Lawrence), also called the Grote Kerk (Great Church). This late-Gothic church, built between 1449 and 1525, was badly damaged during the German bombardment of 1940 but has since been restored and extended. Five black cubes, clad in natural stone, blend with the church's side-elevation. Inside, the church boasts the largest mechanical pipe-organ in Europe. On Tuesdays and Saturdays stalls selling antique coins, stamps and books crowd the Grotekerkplein, the square that surrounds the church.

Cubist apartments

From the back of St Laurens Kerk, turn right onto the wide Binnenrotte, which leads immediately onto the Grote Markt; on most weekdays this wide open space is still the 'great market' of the city, with dozens of stalls selling fresh produce – colourful piles of fruit and vegetables and great bouquets of tulips, daffodils and other flowers in season. It is especially colourful in spring. As the street-sweepers clean up each evening, flocks of hungry herring gulls from the nearby Maas descend squawking to squabble over scraps.

At the southeast side of the Grote Markt is an eye-catching collection of modern architecture, signposted by the brilliant yellow heating ducts which decorate the six stepped storeys of the Rotterdam Biblioteek (Library). South of it stands the remarkable housing complex dominated by the thirteen-storey apartment tower Rotterdammers call Het Potlood (The Pencil), for obvious reasons: it is crowned by a giant conical tip. Around the foot of The Pencil are the mind-bending cubes of the Blaak Heights complex, a dramatic departure from humdrum housing. One of these giddy-looking 'pole dwellings', designed by architect Piet Blom and completed in 1984, is open to visitors.

Barges and cafés

Ahead of you now is the glass canopy of the Rotterdam Blaak Tram and Metro Station, closely resembling a grounded flying saucer. Cross beneath this and turn left, through the road tunnel which traverses the Blaak Heights apartments, and turn promptly right onto Spaanse Kade (Spanish Quay) – so-called because shipping from Spain used to unload here. The quay runs beside the Oude Haven (Old Harbour), which is ringed with more modernistic 'pole dwellings' and by chic open-air café terraces which in summer give it a Mediterranean air. Berthed along the opposite quay is a fleet of traditional Dutch sailing barges that forms the collection of the Openlucht Binnenvaart Museum. The museum also operates the Koningspoort slipway, along the south side of the harbour, where you can see these historic vessels being repaired, maintained and restored.

The banks of the Maas

Keeping the Oude Haven on your right, cross the Spanjaardsbrug (Spaniards' Bridge) to Oudehoofdplein. Immediately ahead of you are the towering crimson suspension piers of the Willemsbrug, spanning the Nieuwe Maas. Cross the Maas Boulevard dual carriageway by means of the zebra crossing and walk beneath the bridge's approach-way to the river bank. Immediately in front of you, suspended above the water, is a striking piece of public art. *Maasbeeld*, by Auke de Vries, completed in 1994, is a cat's-cradle of black metal slabs, rods and twisted bars, 200m (220yd) long.

Walk along the riverside for about 200m (220yd) before turning back towards the northwest, recrossing Maas Boulevard to reach Het Witte Huis (The White House), with its fanciful turrets and elaborate decorative brickwork and stonework. Completed in 1898, this striking building was once Europe's tallest office building, at 45m (148ft); its eleven storeys are now dwarfed by the city's modern office blocks. Below Het Witte Huis, on its southwest side (signposted), you will find the Mariniers Museum der Koninklijke Marine (Royal Marine Museum), which has a collection devoted to the Dutch Marine Corps. The newly independent Dutch Republic can take credit for commissioning the first such force of sea-going soldiers – the Corps was founded in 1665.

From here, turn left along the north side of Wijnhaven (Wine Harbour), where port, brandy, sherry and claret from Oporto and Bordeaux used to be unloaded. The red-painted light-vessel *Beaufort*, moored here, once marked dangerous banks in the North Sea; today, light-vessels have been made redundant by the technology of radar, sonar and satellite-navigation systems.

Walk along Wijnhaven, noting the green-bronze statues which decorate the Posthoornstraat Bridge, to join the north end of the Leuvenhaven, and end your walk at Churchillplein. Alternatively, you could carry straight on from here to start the next walk.

Rotterdam 2: Parks and museums

This walk takes you on a tour of Rotterdam's rich treasury of museums, taking in two picturesque harbours – one of them a haven for historic vessels, the other bobbing with traditional yachts and luxury cruisers – as well as a splash of greenery and a bird's-eye view of the city from the top of its tallest landmark.

Start: Churchillplein Metro; buses 32, 49, trams 3, 6, 7

Finish: Beurs Metro or Churchillplein Metro

Length: 4km (2 $^1/_2$ miles)

Time: 3–4hr, depending on number and length of museum visits

Refreshments: Many cafés and restaurants along the Leuvenhaven and Veerhaven quays, at the Museumpark, and on top of the Euromast tower

Which day: Any day, but note that the Euromast's hours change seasonally – check with Rotterdam VVV office

To visit:
- Prince Hendrik Maritime Museum: same hours as Museumpark (see below) but closed Christmas Day, New Year's Day and April 30
- Open-Air Maritime Museum: Monday–Friday 10.00–12.30 and 13.00–16.00, Sundays 12.00–16.00
- IMAX Waterstad Theatre: IMAX multimedia films at 14.00 and 15.00 daily (for programmes tel 4048844)
- Museum voor Volkenkunde (Museum of Ethnology): same hours as Museumpark (see below) but closed Christmas Day, New Year's Day and April 30
- Euromast: April–September daily 10.00–1900, October–March daily 10.00–17.00, July–August open Tuesday–Saturday until 22.30
- Museumpark (comprising Museum Boymans–van Beuningen, Kunsthal Rotterdam, Rotterdam Natuurmuseum [Natural History Museum], Dutch Institute of Architecture): Tuesday–Saturday 10.00–17.00, Sundays and public holidays 11.00–17.00, closed Mondays (Natural History Museum also closed Saturdays)
- Het Schielandshuis (Rotterdam History Museum): Tuesday–Saturday 10.00–17.00, Sundays and public holidays 13.00–17.00

A historic haven

Leave Churchillplein Metro and walk south, crossing the Westblaak, to reach the Leuvenhaven. At the northwest corner of the harbour you find the Maritime

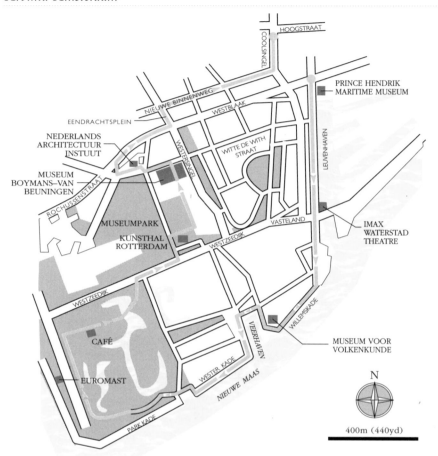

Museum, which was rehoused in this striking modern building in 1986, but has existed since 1874. The museum is named after Prins Hendrik, nicknamed 'The Sailor Prince', who took a great interest in the Dutch Merchant Navy. This is the best place in the Netherlands to savour the flavour of the sea trade on which the country's wealth is based. The richest exhibits are in the museum's Treasure House: they comprise trophies and booty brought home by Dutch adventurers of the Golden Age, who ranged from the East Indies to the Spanish Main. Moored just outside the museum is the restored 19th-century steam cruiser *Buffel*, flagship of a flotilla of historic vessels.

The harbour's west quay is a splendid clutter of maritime equipment, forming the collection of the Open-Air Maritime Museum; tickets are sold in a stubby, red-painted lighthouse on the pier, which is lined with barges, winches, steam cranes and other maritime paraphernalia.

Footsteps of the stars

Leaving the Open-Air Museum, take the short flight of steps on your right up to street-level and turn left onto the Rotterdam Walk of Fame, which leads south along Leuvenhaven to the multimedia IMAX Theatre (Waterstad Theatre). There is a continuous tourist programme every morning to give a taste of the cinema's enormous 23m × 17m (75ft × 56ft) screen and six-channel omnidirectional stereo sound system. Specially made IMAX feature films are shown in the afternoons, then the latest feature films from other sources are shown in the evenings. The handprints and signatures of dozens of celebrities are set in the concrete along the Walk of Fame; among them are B.B. King, the Everly Brothers, Shirley Bassey, Dave Brubeck, Engelbert Humperdinck, Ray Charles, Emmylou Harris, John Denver, Cliff Richard, Johnny Cash and Barry Humphries (Dame Edna Everage).

Highway to the sea

From the IMAX Theatre take the zebra crossing over the Vasteland dual carriageway to Willemskade, the quay which skirts the west side of the outer Leuvenhaven and leads southwest along the north bank of the Nieuwe Maas, Rotterdam's water highway to the sea. To your west, the Nieuwe Maas leads to the vast Europoort complex at the mouth of the river; upstream, it winds its way inland to Gorinchem, where the Waal and the Maas divide.

The Waal in turn wends its way to the German border, where it becomes the Lower Rhine, while the Maas eventually meanders south to Maastricht and Liège in Belgium. These two rivers thus give Rotterdam access to a huge area of Europe. Even today, they carry heavy traffic; before the advent of road and rail transport they were even more vital, and Rotterdam's location made it enormously wealthy.

Along the river and into the trees

On the opposite side of the Leuvenhaven a tall, riveted metal monolith rises from a concrete wave; this is Het Boeg (The Bow), a monument to the courage of the men of the Dutch Merchant Navy during World War II, when many Dutch skippers evaded the German Occupation and took their vessels to aid the Allies. Almost immediately opposite, overlooking the Kop van Zuid harbour on the south bank of the Maas, are the giant twin towers of the Erasmus Bridge. Set for completion in 1996, it has already brought welcome regeneration to the city's docklands. About 1km (half a mile) west of the bridge towers, almost directly opposite you on the south bank of the Nieuwe Maas, is an imposing red-brick building conspicuous for its two green onion-shaped cupolas. This is the former headquarters of the Holland–America Line, the great Dutch transatlantic steamship company; today it is the luxury Hotel New York. The delightful Art Nouveau interior is worth a look, and it is a good place to stop for a snack and a drink on its riverside terrace. To get to it, take the water-taxi from the Veerhaven (see below).

Follow Willemskade, with the river on your left and on your right a row of pretty homes – restored warehouses now turned into up-market apartment buildings. The final building in this row is an attractive confection in pastel yellow stucco, with arched windows, grey wrought-iron balconies on the first and second floors, and an octagonal clock tower.

This is the Museum of Ethnology. Opened more than a century ago, the museum's collection includes fine art, crafts, religious objects and photographs from all over the world. The emphasis, naturally enough, is on former Dutch colonial possessions, and the collections are brought to life by a changing programme of slide shows, music, recordings and films. The museum also hosts a varied weekly programme of music, dance, theatre and song.

Leaving the Museum of Ethnology, turn right and follow the quay around the Veerhaven, where a flotilla of privately owned yachts, graceful schooners and luxury motor cruisers bobs at anchor. From here you can catch a water-taxi across the river to the luxury Hotel New York, a landmark in its own right.

Detour back to the Veerhaven and follow the quay round to the river front, which now becomes become Wester Kade, a leafy esplanade which is at its prettiest in spring and early summer when its many cherry and magnolia trees are in bloom. Wester Kade in turn becomes Park Kade, at its junction with Westerlaan; cross Westerlaan to enter the lush greenery of Park de Heuvel, beside the stylized granite statue dubbed Wilhelmina, at the park's eastern corner.

In summer the park is a delightful place for unstructured wandering. There are swards of neatly trimmed grass on which to sunbathe, shady trees, serpentine lakes full of coots and dabchicks, and a pleasant café-terrace beside the northern arm of the lake. Overlooking the park – and the whole of the city – is the space-age obelisk of the Euromast. To reach the tower, follow the Heuvellaan Path around the perimeter to the Heuvelbrug, then turn left and cross the bridge to the tower entrance.

Soar into space

Built in 1960 as a visitor attraction, the Euromast is an experience in itself. First you take a high-speed lift to the Space Platform, 100m (330ft) up. There, rocket engines and lighting effects mimic a real rocket launch and, rotating slowly, you climb into orbit at 185m (607ft). When the nearby medical faculty of the university was completed in 1968, it topped the Euromast by 7m (23ft), so a second stage was added to the Euromast to take it to its present height.

Back on earth, probably breathless, recross the Heuvelbrug and walk through the park to leave it by the northern corner, rejoining the street on Westzeedijk at its junction with Kievitslaan. Immediately opposite you as you leave the park are the white Modernist blocks of the Erasmus University. The tower of the medical faculty, 114m (374ft) tall, is a Rotterdam landmark; built in 1965–68 and designed by A. Hagoort, G. Martens and J. Prouve, it has a concrete frame clad entirely in white enamelled aluminium panels. It was built in record time, and made revolutionary use of prefabrication. The lower block looks like nothing so much as a giant multi-deck train poised to move off.

Around the museums

Cross Westzeedijk and follow the green signpost labelled 'Natuurmuseum, Museumpark, Museum Boymans', which directs you down a flight of steps to a sunken access-way leading to the Rotterdam Kunsthal. Cut across the terrace of the Kunsthal's café-restaurant Domus Artis into the Museumpark.

The Natuurmuseum (Natural History Museum) is signposted and is 50m (55yd) to your left. If you are not tempted by its rather pedestrian collection of stuffed birds, animals and reptiles, carry on through the park to its north side, and at the northeast corner enter the Museum Boymans–van Beuningen, a two-storey brick building housing four excellent collections: old paintings and sculpture; modern classics and contemporary art; applied art and design; prints and drawings. Among the old masters exhibited are Pieter Brueghel (*c*.1520–1569), Hieronymus Bosch (*c*.1460–1516) and Rembrandt. Da Vinci, Dürer, Cézanne and Picasso prints, plus works by Salvador Dali, Vincent Van Gogh and Karel Appel, are also displayed.

Just south of the museum is a sculpture garden – look out for the surreal, curving giant screw by the decorative pool.

From the Museum Boymans–van Beuningen, cross the northern Museumpark access-road to the striking Nederlands Architectuur Instuut (Dutch Institute of Architecture). This vast glass box, surrounded by water and supported by a giant steel skeleton, is one of the largest centres of architectural excellence in the world – appropriate for a city that places a high value on its treasury of adventurous post-war architecture.

Walk to the back (north) of the Instuut building and turn right along Rockhussenstraat, walking for some 500m (550yd) to Eendrachtsplein. Cross this busy little square and turn right again from its northeast corner along Oude Binnenweg, a pedestrianized shopping street which quickly leads you back to Coolsingel.

Turn right into Korte Hoogstraat. At no. 31 enter the outstandingly pretty Schielandshuis, a palatial 17th-century mansion with an ornate stucco façade and portico which houses the Rotterdam History Museum, which has a collection of art and artifacts celebrating the city from its earliest days. Pride of place is given to the Atlas van Stolk, one of the earliest world atlases, dating from the Golden Age of Dutch overseas expansion and exploration.

After visiting the History Museum, retrace your steps to Coolsingel, then turn right to reach Beurs Metro Station, which is 75m (83yd) up Coolsingel and marks the end of your walk.

Haarlem 1: The Grote Markt and Flemish Haarlem

*Haarlem, capital of the province of North Holland, is just under 20km (16 miles)
from Amsterdam. It is a compact city of 150,000 souls, and the medieval city-centre
has escaped the sometimes brash tourist development and red-light sleaze of central
Amsterdam. Haarlem is the nexus of the Dutch bulb industry, and on a spring trip
from the city you pass through wide fields of brilliantly coloured tulips and daffodils.
Like Amsterdam, Haarlem boomed in the 17th century and is built within a
concentric system of canal rings. It is close to the coast; the beach resort of
Zandvoort and the nearby national park are popular summergetaways for
Amsterdam city-dwellers.
The first of our two Haarlem walks takes you through the medieval heart of the city;
for a longer walk you can combine it with our second tour, which takes in a choice of
Haarlem's museums and monuments (see page 116).*

Start/finish: Haarlem Stationsplein; trains to and from Amsterdam Centraal
Station every 10–15 minutes (journey-time 15–20 minutes)

Length: 4.8km (3 miles)

Time: 2½hr

Refreshments: Plenty of taverns and restaurants around the Grote Markt,
Haarlem's medieval central square, and a surprisingly charming
station restaurant which has been restored to pristine
19th-century condition

Which day: Not Sundays

To visit:
- Sint Anthonieskerk (Church of St Anthony of Padua):
  Monday–Saturday 08.00–16.00
- Corrie Ten Boom Huis: Tuesday–Saturday 10.00–16.00,
  November 1–April 30 11.00–15.00
- Stadbuis (Town Hall): Monday–Friday 08.30–17.00
- Haarlem Archaeological Museum: daily 13.00–17.00
- Frans Hals Museum: Monday–Saturday 11.00–17.00,
  Sunday 13.00–17.00
- Sint Bavokerk (St Bavo's Church): daily 10.00–16.00
- Waalse Kerk: Monday–Saturday 08.00–16.00
- Janskerk: Monday–Saturday 08.00–16.00

Many of Haarlem's most outstanding buildings are the work of Flemish master-
builders who fled to the city from the south (now Belgium) in the 16th and 17th
centuries to escape Spanish oppression and religious persecution. Earlier, many

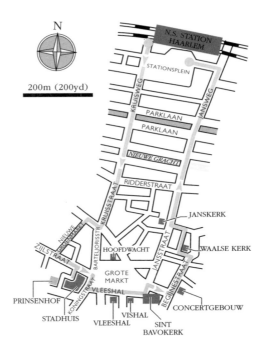

Haarlemmers had perished when the city had been besieged by the Spanish Duke of Alva, in 1572–3, and so the city welcomed these new arrivals, most of whom were wealthy traders and manufacturers.

Painters and architects

At the time, the free cities of the newly independent Netherlands actively competed to attract these rich immigrants to help rebuild their fortunes after the ravages of the Spanish wars. Haarlem was among the most successful in this enterprise, and by the 1620s more than half its people were of Flemish origin. One of them was the portraitist Frans Hals, Haarlem's most famous resident; another was the architect Lieven de Key (*c*.1560–1627), who left his stamp on the entire city-centre. The surviving buildings and layout of 16th- and 17th-century Haarlem are strongly reminiscent of medieval Flemish cities such as Ghent or Bruges.

Before you leave the Stationsplein, take time to have a look at the grand front of the station. Like Amsterdam Centraal, this was built during the heyday of the steam train, and its decorative towers are pretty rather than functional. Leaving the Stationsplein, turn left onto Kruisweg, cross the Parklaan and Nieuwe Gracht canal, and walk straight on down Kruisstraat.

On your right, where this street becomes Bartel Joris Straat, is the Hofje van Oorschot. The hidden courtyards of 15th-century almshouses like this one are a feature of Haarlem's town-centre.

At the end of Kruisstraat, turn right, cross the Krocht and turn left into Nieuwe Groenmarkt. The prominent church of St Anthony of Padua, which you find here, was built by the Flemish architect Tilman François Suys (1783–1861), one of the architects of the Mozes en Aaronkerk on the Waterlooplein in Amsterdam (see page 32). The statues and altars are by Pieter Jozef de Cuyper.

At the corner of Nieuwe Groenmarkt and Zijlstraat, turn left to walk towards the Grote Markt, Haarlem's medieval centrepiece – but, before you reach the square, detour briefly to the right into 't Pand. Pass through a prominent gateway which leads you into the Prinsenhof, laid out in 1721 as a medicinal herb garden. In the middle of the square is a statue of Laurens Janszoon Coster (*c.*1370–1440), believed (if only by his compatriots) to have invented movable type. The idea threatened the 15th-century Church's monopoly of the printed word: Coster was accused of sorcery and had to leave town for Germany, where he may have passed on his ideas to Johannes Gutenberg (1400–1468), more widely credited as movable type's inventor. A second statue of Coster stands in the Grote Markt.

As Zijlstraat joins the Grote Markt on the square's northwest corner, sidetrack briefly left into Bartel Joris Straat; cross to the east side of the street to visit the Corrie Ten Boom House, also called the Hiding Place, at no. 19. The Ten Boom family moved into the street in 1837, when Willem Ten Boom opened a clock and watch shop. His son Casper took over the business, and the house later passed to Casper's daughter Corrie. Devout Christians, during World War II the family sheltered Jewish refugees and members of the Dutch Resistance, and their home became a centre for a network of underground contacts. On 28 February 1944 the Ten Booms were betrayed and the Gestapo raided the house, arresting six of the family. Casper, then aged 84, Betsie (59) and Christiaan (49) died as prisoners, while another family member, Willem (50), survived the war only to die of exhaustion. Four Jewish refugees and two Resistance members hidden behind a false wall in Corrie's bedroom were missed by the Gestapo; after two and a half days without food or water they escaped. Corrie herself survived the Ravensbruck concentration camp. In 1988 the house was reopened as a museum, exhibiting documents, photographs and other mementos. A plaque outside commemorates the family's four martyrs. A guided tour of the house takes about 45 minutes.

Leaving the Corrie Ten Boom House, turn left and walk back down Bartel Joris Straat to the Grote Markt.

The Grote Markt

Haarlem's main square has changed little since France Hals painted its portrait in the 17th century, and is still dominated by impressive medieval buildings. Arriving from the northwest corner of the square, turn right for an anti-clockwise tour.

Occupying the entire west side of the Grote Markt between Zijlstraat and Koningstraat is the Stadhuis (Town Hall). The building has been altered and added to over centuries. The oldest parts were built during the 14th century as a hunting lodge for the counts of Holland and a neighbouring Dominican monastery.

After the great fire of 1351, which destroyed much of the city, Count William V built the section now known as the Count's Hall and used as the city's gala reception room; it is open to the public. Hanging from the ceiling is a gaping whale's jaw brought back by the Haarlem captain Jan van Linschoten (1563–1611) from his voyage of exploration to the Arctic islands of Novaya Zemlya in 1595. Around the hall are 21 panels portraying the counts and countesses of Holland. The series is called *The Dance of Death*, and ends with a typically gruesome medieval portrayal of Death, intended to remind the city's rulers that their worldly power, wealth and glory were merely transitory. The paintings are 16th-century copies of earlier monastery frescoes.

During the 15th century the builders added several more halls along the Zijlstraat side of the building, as well as the Vierschaar (High Courtroom) where public judgement was pronounced. At the same time, a bell-tower was added, though the existing tower is the most recent part of the building, having been added in 1913. The Zijlstraat wing houses a 17th-century tapestry, done by the Flemish weaver Joseph Thienpoint of Oudenaerde, which depicts the capture of Damiate in Egypt by crusaders from Haarlem in 1219; Haarlem is still so proud of this achievement that a special carillon is rung every night to commemorate it.

Towards the end of the 16th century the Town Hall was largely destroyed by fire, and the newly appointed city architect, Lieven de Key, was commissioned to rebuild it. De Key, a Fleming who had fled to England, came back to Haarlem in 1593, and many of the buildings around the Grote Markt bear his stamp. The great staircase which leads to the Count's Hall is his work, as are the monumental salons of the Zijlstraat wing of the Town Hall. In 1633 he radically modernized the façade of the building, endowing it with its stylish Italian Renaissance elements. The five coloured poles standing in the Grote Markt outside are a memorial to De Key by sculptor Roger Raveel. Erected in 1990, they vary in height and are intended to echo De Key's finely proportioned perspectives. One wonders what the 16th-century architect would have thought of them.

Medieval market halls

Leaving the Town Hall, cross Koningstraat at the southwest corner of the square. Midway along the south side of the Grote Markt stands another of De Key's buildings, the Vleeshal (Meat Hall). Built in 1603, it is a fine example of Dutch Renaissance architecture. Today it houses the Haarlem Archaeological Museum and an annexe of the Frans Hals Museum (see page 119). The high gables are, bearing in mind the building's original purpose, appropriately adorned with the carved heads of sheep and oxen. Diagonally opposite the Vleeshal is the Vishal (Fish Hall), built in 1768 to replace the town's 17th-century fish market. It too is now used as an exhibition annexe of the Frans Hals Museum.

Between the two buildings, close to the top of Warmoesstraat, a small statue of knights in combat is a reminder that the square was not only a marketplace but, on feast days, a tournament venue where the counts and their subjects could watch displays of martial skill.

The Great Church

The most prominent building on the Grote Markt, now right in front of you, is the great Gothic Church of St Bavo, another reminder of the Flemish connection – it shares its patron saint with Sint Baafs in Ghent.

The church was built between 1370 and 1520, and is a late Gothic cruciform basilica with a slender wooden tower. Evert Spowater, master builder of Antwerp, oversaw the addition of the graceful transept between 1445 and 1465; the Renaissance font chapel on the south side was modernized by de Key in 1593, one of his first commissions as city architect.

With its white arched windows and its softly coloured stonework, the light interior of the church is one of the prettiest in the Netherlands. It is dominated by a splendid organ, ornamented in gilt and crimson and built by the famous Amsterdam organ-maker Christian Muller in 1738. With 64 registers and 5000 pipes, this is one of the largest church organs in the world. Among its admirers were George Friederic Handel (1685–1759) and the young Wolfgang Amadeus Mozart (1756–1791), who played here during the course of his tour of the Low Countries in 1766.

Look out for the brass lectern, dating from 1499, and the brass choir screen, dating from 1509, both of them the work of a Mechlin metalsmith, Jan Fierens. In the choir is the grave of Frans Hals; and on the way out, by the exit, is the tombstone of Pieter Saenredam (1597–1695), whose delightful paintings of Dutch church interiors are so perfectly executed that they are still used as guides for restoration work.

Facing you across the cobbled square as you exit the church is a decorative building rather like a miniature castle – the Hoofdwacht. The Hoofdwacht has a long and venerable history of law and order: today it is the city police station; in the 17th and 18th centuries it was the headquarters of the Haarlem City Watch. From St Bavo's, turn right, then left to walk up Begijnestraat.

A choral revival

On your right is the pompous building of the Concertgebouw, built in 1885; its long-standing choral tradition was revived just after World War I by yet another Flemish visitor, Lieven Defosel, the famous choirmaster of Bruges. At the end of Begijnstraat, turn left on Begijnsteeg, then almost immediately right onto the Begijnhof.

A short way up this narrow street, on your right, is the Waalse Kerk (Walloon Church), a medieval church which became a place of worship for Huguenot émigrés from France and for French-speaking (Walloon) expatriates from the southern provinces of the Low Countries. The façade, dating from 1670, is graced by a doorway surmounted by festoons of fruit and flowers and topped off with a triangular pediment. Follow the Begijnhof to its northern end, turn left, and walk along to Jansstraat. Opposite you is the Janskerk, originally a monastery church of the Knights of St John, dating back to the 14th and 15th centuries. Geertgen tot Sint Jans (1460–1495), who lived here, was among the 15th-century painters who began to change the scope of Dutch painting to include narrative elements and a less rigid composition. Geertgen's paintings are still very clearly religious art, highly stylized and verging on the iconic, but his colours are vivid, adding a liveliness to the stilted figures. Once again, Lieven de Key added his portion to the earlier building, in the shape of a small tower dating from 1595. From here, walk back along Jansstraat, across Nieuwe Gracht and along Jansweg to return to Stationsplein.

Alternatively, turn right on Korte Jansstraat to link up with the next walk.

Haarlem 2: Museums and monuments

This walk takes you through the oldest part of Haarlem and around its canals, stopping at some of the city's fascinating museums. The high point is a visit to the Frans Hals Museum, where some of the 16th-century master's greatest works are displayed.

Start/finish:	Stationsplein; trains from Amsterdam Centraal Station
Length:	6km (4 miles)
Time:	3 ¹/₂ hr (including 1hr for the Frans Hals Museum)
Refreshments:	See Haarlem 1, page 110
Which day:	Tuesday–Friday if you want to catch all of the museums
To visit:	● Bakenesserhofje: Monday–Friday 10.00–17.00
	● Teylers Museum: Tuesday–Saturday 10.00–17.00, Sundays and public holidays 13.00–17.00
	● ABC Architectuurcentrum/South Kennemerland Historical Museum: Tuesday–Saturday 12.00–17.00, Sunday 13.00–17.00
	● Frans Hals Museum: Monday–Saturday 11.00–17.00, Sunday 13.00–17.00

Turn left out of the station, pausing for a moment to admire the bronze by Kees Verkade of the Haarlem Flower Girls, in the middle of the Stationsplein. Leave the square by its east side. Turn right, walk down Jansweg, crossing Nieuwe Gracht by the Jansbrug; turn left into Korte Jansstraat, then right onto Bakenessergracht.

Goldsmiths and almshouses

The houses either side of this narrow canal are among the oldest in Haarlem. Look out for historic gablestones, like the one at no. 9, where two crowned acorns are a reminder of the fact that in the 17th century the building was a well-known brewery. A short way down the canal, detour right into Goudsmidspleintje (Little Goldsmiths' Square), where a gablestone with a gold chalice relief marks the former guildhouse of the city's gold- and silversmiths. The inscription below reads Dit is de Gout Smits Camer (This is the Goldsmiths' Chamber).

Back on the canal, continue to your right to the Bakenesserhofje (entrance on Wijde Appelaarsteeg, around the corner), one of about twenty almshouse-courtyards in Haarlem. These almshouse foundations are divided into three kinds – Church hofjes, mainly for beguines (or begijns; lay nuns) of the Church; foundation hofjes, built by Church councils or by wealthy philanthropists to house the poor and needy; and hofjes set up by the city guilds to shelter indigent members and their dependents. The Bakenesserhofje, founded in 1395, is claimed to be the oldest almshouse in the Netherlands.

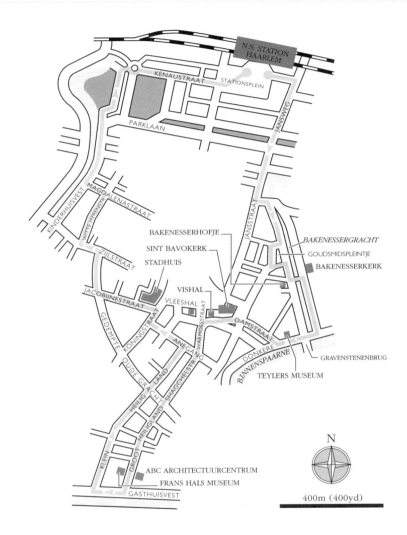

Cross the canal by the bridge at the end of Korte Begijnstraat for a closer look at the Bakenesserkerk, built in the 15th century and restored in 1972.

Bakenessergracht opens onto the River Spaarne, which winds its way through Haarlem and forms the boundary of the medieval town. Turn right across the Wildemansbrug, at the mouth of the canal. On your left, the picturesque Gravenstenenbrug drawbridge crosses the Spaarne. Just behind it is the twin façade of the 17th-century Oliphant Brewery – according to a 1623 tax roll there were more than fifty breweries in the city. The Spaarne provided a supply of clear water for brewing, and, as in Amsterdam and elsewhere in the Netherlands, beer was the preferred alternative to drinking the foul water of the city canals. The tyrannical Duke of Alva, the Spanish regent who besieged the city in 1572–3, punished the defeated Haarlemmers by drowning them in the Spaarne, tied together back-to-back.

A haphazard collection

Walk on a few tens of metres along the west bank of the Spaarne to the Teylers Museum, at no. 16 Spaarne.

The museum, founded in the late 18th century, is the oldest in the Netherlands, with a grand, haphazard collection of everything from fossils and semi-precious stones to old brass astronomical instruments and microscopes, coins and medals, dinosaur skeletons, prints and paintings, including works by Rembrandt, Raphael and Michelangelo, and eccentric pieces of experimental machinery whose purpose is now almost forgotten.

The museum interior is worth seeing in its own right, with its polished woodwork and gleaming brass. It is a reminder of an age when science was less the province of specialists and theorists and more the playground of anyone with an inquiring mind. Haarlem owes the museum to Pieter Teyler van der Hulst, one of its wealthier citizens. Having made a fortune in the weaving and spinning industry, he bequeathed it to create a Foundation dedicated to the arts and sciences. The museum's oldest room, the Oval Room, opened in 1784. Over the next two centuries the Teyler expanded to house its growing collection. The striking Neoclassical façade dates from 1878. A new wing is planned to take the venerable institution into the 21st century.

Walk on along the Spaarne to the corner of Damstraat, where a solid-looking building faced with blocks of natural stone stands out in this city of brick façades. The Waag, or Weighhouse, is attributed to the ubiquitous Lieven de Key, city architect in the late 16th and 17th centuries, who planned or added to most of the city's public buildings. This one was built in 1597–8.

Shopping for antiques

Turn right on Damstraat and walk towards the back of the St Bavokerk (see page 114), then curve left across the Oude Groenmarkt and turn onto Warmoesstraat, a shopping street with a mosaic pavement; if you look around, you will realize that the mosaics indicate the wares on sale in the shops nearby. These are very varied, with here an antiquarian bookseller, there a fashionable boutique or antiques store. Continuing down what has now become Schagchelstraat, you'll find musical-instrument makers, watchmakers, costumiers . . . At Bonnette, no. 32 Schagchelstraat, you can sample and buy some of the fine chocolates for which Haarlem is famous. The city is the home of the Droste chocolate company. Across Gedempte Oude Gracht, Schagchelstraat becomes Groot Heiligland; the stepped-gable houses at nos. 17–21 and nos. 18–22 were the original Sint Elisabeth City Hospital, built in 1610.

No. 47 Groot Heiligland houses the ABC Architectuurcentrum, a venue for exhibitions on architecture and landscaping; unless you have a special interest in the subject, it is not worth more than a very quick look. However, housed in the same building is the more generally interesting South Kennemerland History Museum, which gives an interesting insight into traditional farm and town life, the growth of the huge bulb-farming industry and the battle against the sea.

But the high point of this walk is in the building opposite, at no. 62 Groot Heiligland.

Haarlem's greatest painter

The grand 17th-century building which now houses the Frans Hals Museum was built as one of the city's hofjes, originally an old men's home, designed (predictably) by Lieven de Key. In the 19th century it was a city orphanage. The Haarlem municipality bought it in 1906, added two new wings and restored the rest, and laid out a 17th-century garden and inner courtyard.

The museum is by no means monopolized by Hals, though it does have more than twenty of his paintings. A number of his 17th-century contemporaries are exhibited as well, and the extensive modern collection provides a welcome contrast to the great portrait painter's dark canvases. The Restoration Workshop allows visitors to see the slow, painstaking toil that goes into removing centuries of grime to bring an old masterpiece back to pristine condition. If you have already visited the Grote Markt, you'll be struck by Hals's painting of it as it was in the 17th century: the square is essentially unchanged!

Hals was among the greatest of portraitists, and was much in demand as a painter of group portraits of militia companies and city worthies. Like Rembrandt, he was capable of imbuing his portraits with what can seem like sly comment on the character of the sitter, just this side of caricature. Look at the faces in the group portraits of the *Civic Guard of St Adrian* (1633) or the *Regents of the Old Mens' Home* (1664).

Frans Hals was born in Antwerp in 1581 and came to Haarlem with his family ten years later, when many Flemish Protestants were moving north. He was highly successful as a painter of Haarlem's civic élite, but like his contemporary Rembrandt he died poor. He was an unrepentant drinker and reveller, with an incurable taste for the low-life, even when president of the Haarlem Painters' Guild. He had ten legitimate children and a number of illegitimate ones, and sank steadily deeper into debt until in 1664 he was virtually bankrupt. A grateful town council, however, recognizing his talents, paid his rent and gave him a pension of 200 guilders a year. Some stories claim that he ended his days in the very almshouse building which is now his museum, but there is no evidence for this. He died in 1666, aged 81, outliving most of his contemporaries, which suggests his bohemian lifestyle can have done him little harm.

His works are grouped in what is sensibly enough called the Frans Hals Room. The museum's collection of works by other 16th- and 17th-century painters includes masterpieces by Floris van Dyck (1575–1651), Jan Mostaert (*c.*1475–*c.*1555), Hendrick Cornelisz and Jan van Scorel (1495–1562).

From the museum, turn right at the end of Groot Heiligland onto the Gasthuisvest canal-side. Walk up one block and turn right onto Klein Heiligland. No. 64 Klein Heiligland is another 18th-century hospice, the Hospital of Our Lady and St Anthony, but its courtyard is not open to the public. The gateway next to no. 29 is called the Omvalspoort (Reeling Gateway); subsiding foundations have pitched it at a drunken angle, and it is supported by the buildings on either side.

Klein Heiligland becomes Frankestraat after it crosses Gedempte Oude Gracht; there is a good view of St Bavokerk and its tower as you walk up this street. Turn left into Anegang, which is Haarlem's main shopping area, and cross Grote Houtstraat. Turn right onto Koningstraat and, just as you reach the south side of the Stadhuis, turn left on Jacobijnestraat. At no. 3 there is a fine façade dating from 1662; the building is called In den gulden Salm (The House of the Golden Salmon). Next door, at no. 1, is the former sampling-house of the Haarlem bakers' guild.

Statues and almshouses

Turn right onto Gedempte Oude Gracht, walk past the Post Office on your left, and turn left shortly afterwards onto Zijlstraat. The statue opposite no. 29 is of Johan van Oldenbarneveldt, the 16th-century statesman and legislator. Turn right here, into the Witte Herenstraat. Several of Haarlem's many almshouses are located along this street: the Comanshof at no. 32, Frans Loenen Hofje at no. 24 and the rather drab Lutherse Hofje at no. 12.

At the north end of Witte Herenstraat, turn left into the Magdalenastraat, then right along Kinderhuisvest, the east bank of the Leidsevaart Canal. Cross Nieuwe Gracht by the Manegebrug, and bear right to walk through the canal-side Kenaupark, a welcome green space on the edge of the city-centre. The statue in the middle of the park is of a heroine of the Dutch Resistance during World War II, Hannie Schaft.

Leaving the park, turn right into the Kenaustraat, which leads you back to Stationsplein and the end of this walk.

Plate 25: *The picturesque Wildemansbrug drawbridge crosses the River Spaarne in the centre of Haarlem (see the Haarlem 2: Museums and monuments walk, page 117).*

Plate 26: *A typical scene by one of Delft's maze of small canals (see the Delft walk, page 121).*

Plate 27: *At Gouda's weekly summer cheese-market, dairy farmers bring their great rounds of cheese to the Markt square (see the Gouda walk, page 126).*

Plate 28: Utrecht's unusual sunken canal is unique to the city (see the Utrecht walk, page 133).

Plate 29: The Neoclassical façade of the Brouchoven hofje, one of Leiden's many pretty almshouses (see the Leiden 2: City almshouses walk, page 143).

Plate 30: The De Put Windmill is an authentic reconstruction of the mill built in 1619 by Jan Janszoon Put (see the Leiden 1: Young Rembrandt walk, page 135).

Plate 31: *Rembrandt would have looked out every day to the gabled front of the Stadstimmerwerf (Town Carpenters' Wharf), opposite his family home (see the Leiden 1: Young Rembrandt walk, page 135).*

Plate 32: *With its avenues of vivid flowers, the Keukenhof in spring is one of Holland's loveliest sights (see the Keukenhof walk, page 152).*

Delft

Delft is virtually a suburb of The Hague, only 8km (5 miles) and five minutes away by train, and is not very much further from Rotterdam, which is 11km (7 miles) away. Among the prettiest small towns in the Netherlands, Delft has many narrow canals criss-crossed by little wrought-iron footbridges. Most are also lined with lime trees, and this walk is at its best in summer when the town-centre is full of greenery. This short walk takes in the highlights of the town-centre.

Although Delft has been settled since the 11th century, much of the city burned in the great fire of 1536, and most landmarks date from the 16th-century rebuilding. Also in the 16th century, a canal was built linking Delft with the sea by way of the Maas estuary. The harbour at Delfshaven was owned by Delft until it was swallowed up by Rotterdam in 1886.

Start/finish:	Stationsplein; trains from Amsterdam (change at The Hague) run twice hourly; journey-time is about 1hr
Length:	6km (3½ miles)
Time:	2hr
Refreshments:	Cafés along the route and in the Markt
To visit:	● Het Prinsenhof: Tuesday-Saturday 10.00–17.00, Sunday 13.00–17.00
	● Museum Lambert van Meerten: Tuesday–Saturday 10.00–17.00, Sunday 13.00–17.00
	● Oude Kerk: Monday–Saturday 09.00–17.00
	● Nieuwe Kerk: April–October Monday–Saturday 09.00–18.00, November–March Monday–Saturday 11.00–16.00
	● Museum Paul Tetar van Elven: Tuesday–Saturday 10.00–17.00, Sunday 13.00–17.00

With the railway behind you, turn left out of Stationsplein and walk up Westvest. Where it joins Phoenixstraat and Hugo de Grootstraat, turn right along the first small canal, the Binnenwater, and walk along Binnenwatersluis to its junction with the Koornmarkt. Turn left and walk along the Oude Delft, the city's oldest canal – indeed, the first urban canal in the Netherlands – to Delft's most important historic building, the Prinsenhof (Prince's Court), which you find on your left on St Agathaplein, a pretty square that is surrounded by spreading chestnut trees.

Built as the Convent of St Agatha in the early 15th century, the building looks far from martial, although it was William the Silent's headquarters during his struggle with Spain. William took over the building in 1572 and lived here for twelve years until, in 1584, he was gunned down by one Balthasar Gérards, who had been urged on by a pro-Spanish priest who promised him absolution for the act. The assassination did the Spanish cause no good. William was succeeded as Stadhouder by

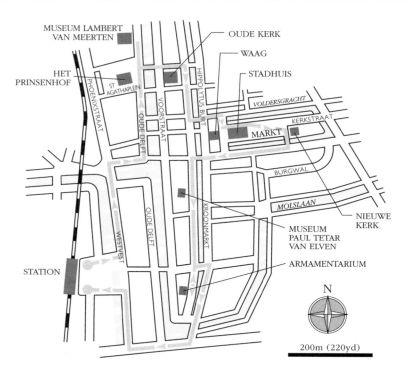

his son Maurice of Nassau, who proved an even more capable leader and general.

The Prinsenhof is now a museum devoted to the history of the Dutch Republic, complete with a gallery of paintings of smoke-clouded naval battles, cavalry charges and helmeted pikemen. The most interesting part is the exhibition on William himself in the former royal apartments. In the Moordhal (Murder Hall), where William was assassinated, you can see two holes said to have been made by the assassin's bullets.

Tiles and a leaning tower

Leaving the museum, walk back across the St Agathaplein and turn left to walk less than one block up the Oude Delft to the Museum Lambert van Meerten, at no. 119. In this prettily preserved 19th-century house are exhibited hundreds of 17th- and 18th-century Delft tiles.

The town began producing hand-painted copies of blue-and-white glazed Chinese porcelain as early as the 16th century, but the potters of Delft were eventually forced out of the market by cheaper chinaware mass-produced in England. More than 80 per cent of all the so-called 'Delftware' now sold by the ton to visiting tourists is in fact made in Gouda, more famous for its cheese.

Now cross the Oude Delft diagonally to the next landmark on this walk, the leaning tower of the Oude Kerk. The tiled tower supports the heaviest church bell in the Netherlands, weighing almost 9000kg (20,000 pounds). One wonders how long it will be before the whole drunken edifice tumbles into the canal. The carillon is rung only on royal occasions.

Among those buried in the church are two great Dutch admirals. Admiral Maerten Tromp (1597–1653) was famous for his audacious raids into English waters during the sea-wars with the British in the second half of the 17th century. As a boy, Tromp was press-ganged by English pirates, which probably contributed to his dislike of the English as well as his sea-fighting skills. Tromp dared to take his fleet right into the Thames estuary, and is said to have displayed a broom lashed to his ship's flagstaff as a sign that he meant to sweep the seas clean of English ships. In the end, however, they swept the seas clear of him; he was killed in an engagement with the English Admiral George Monk (1608–1670) off the Gabbaard. Nearby lies Admiral Piet Heyn (1578–1629), another great naval leader during the wars against Spain.

On a more peaceful note, Jan Vermeer (1632–1675) is also buried here. With Rembrandt and Frans Hals, Vermeer was one of the greatest painters of the 17th century, recognized especially for his portrayals of Dutch domesticity. Unlike most of his contemporaries, he was far from prolific, producing fewer then forty paintings in his relatively short life. Rembrandt lived to be 63 and the reprobate Hals to be 81, but Vermeer died at 42. The church is noted also for its twenty-six splendid stained-glass windows by Joep Nicolaas.

The New Church

Walk on past the Oude Kerk to the Hippolytus Burt, cross it, and turn right to walk down to the Markt, the central square of the old town. At the Waag – the former town weigh-house – turn left, then right, and walk past the Stadhuis and diagonally across the square to reach the 14th-century Nieuwe Kerk (New Church), where almost all the princes and kings of the House of Orange are buried. Within the church is the massive black and white marble sarcophagus of William the Silent, surrounded by splendid marble columns flecked with gold and overlooked by glorious stained-glass windows depicting the later triumphs of his House. His marble effigy rests on top of the sarcophagus, with his faithful pet dog lying at his feet. The tomb was designed by the Amsterdam architects Hendrick and Pieter de Keyser, who between them designed most of Amsterdam's great 17th-century churches and steeples.

Facing the church across the Markt square is the Stadhuis (Town Hall). Walk past the statue of Hugo Grotius, the Delft-born father of modern international law, and pause to admire the Stadhuis's bright red painted shutters and gilt mouldings. The building is in the 17th-century Dutch Renaissance style, but has an earlier 13th-century prison tower.

Leaving the Markt behind you, and with the Town Hall on your right, walk along the Oude Langedijk and turn left as you reach the Koornmarkt. Walk down its right-hand side to no. 67, where you will find the Museum Paul Tetar van Elven. Tetar, a 19th-century imitator of Vermeer, left his gracious 18th-century mansion, including its splendid collection of period furniture, Delftware and paintings, to the nation. His own competent but uninspired works bear no comparison with those of his hero or others of his illustrious contemporaries.

Continue down the Koornmarkt to Langegeer and the Armamentarium (Military Museum), a solid-looking building which has a red-tiled roof and is surrounded on three sides by water. This was the 17th-century city armoury: cannon, powder and shot could be loaded and unloaded from canal barges directly into its store-rooms. It now houses a comprehensive exhibition of Dutch military history, weapons, maps and other ephemera related to the wars against Spain and the Holy Roman Empire.

From the museum, cross the Koornmarkt to the Langegeer, turn right, and at the end of the block turn right again to return to Stationsplein.

Gouda

Gouda is everybody's idea of a typical Dutch town. A ring of canals surrounds the pretty 15th-century town-centre, with its Gothic buildings.

Start/finish:	Stationsplein; frequent trains to and from Amsterdam Centraal Station (journey-time 45 minutes)
Length:	5km (3.2 miles)
Time:	1–2hr
Refreshments:	Cafés and restaurants around the Markt – don't forget to sample treacle-filled Gouda waffles, the sticky and satisfying local delicacy
Which day:	Not Mondays

To visit:

- Cheese and Old Crafts Market: July–August Thursday mornings
- Exposeum Goudse Kaaswaag (Waag Cheese Museum); April–October, Tuesday–Saturday 10.00–17.00, Sunday 12.00–17.00
- Stadhuis: Tuesday–Saturday 10.00–17.00
- Grote of Sint Janskerk (Great or St John's Church): Monday–Saturday 09.00–17.00
- Stedelijk Museum Het Catharina Gasthuis (St Catherine's Hospice Museum): Tuesday–Saturday 10.00–17.00, Sunday 12.00–17.00
- Stedelijk Museum De Moriaan (Blackamoor Municipal Museum): Tuesday–Saturday 10.00–17.00, Sunday 12.00–17.00
- Adrie Moerings Goudse Pottebakkerij en Pijpenmakerij (Pipemakers): Monday–Friday 09.00–17.00, Saturday 11.00–17.00
- Binnenhaven Museum (Canal Harbour Museum): Tuesday–Saturday 10.00–17.00, Sunday 12.00–17.00
- Molen De Roode Leeuw (Red Lion Mill): Tuesday–Saturday 09.00–17.00
- Zuidhollands Verzetsmuseum (South Holland Resistance Museum): Tuesday–Saturday 10.00–17.00, Sunday 12.00–17.00

Gouda's railway station lies in the modern part of town, outside the ring of canals which makes the medieval town-centre into an island. With the Stationsplein behind you, turn left onto the Vredebest, which angles southeast to Kleiwegplein. Follow the Kleiweg south across the canal; after the Kleiweg has become Hoogstraat, turn left into the Markt, the medieval square at the heart of Gouda.

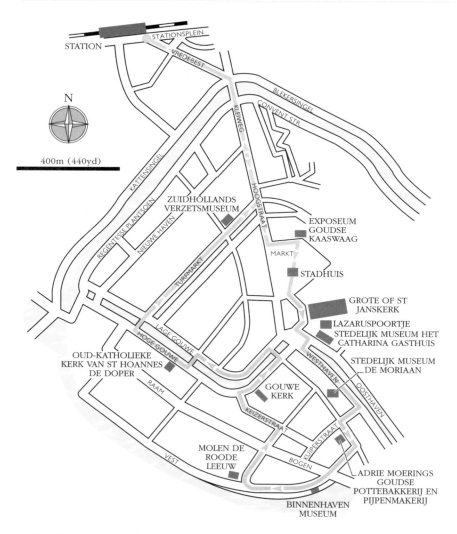

Gouda grew up at the junction of the Ijssel and Gouwe rivers, and was one of the first Dutch communities to be granted the privileges of a city, with a charter from Count Floris V of Holland in the 13th century.

Say cheese

At Markt no. 36, the Waag (Weighhouse) is the symbol of a town associated in so many visitors' minds with fine Dutch cheese. Built by the architect Pieter Post (1608–1669) in 1668, it is still the centre of the weekly summer cheese-market

(Thursday mornings in July and August), when dairy farmers from the surrounding countryside bring in their great rounds of yellow cheese to the Markt square to be weighed and sold.

The Classical Baroque building, with its six doorways, is now the Waag Cheese Exposeum, a museum which uses brand new electronics and interactive audio–visual media to tell the visitor about the age-old craft of cheesemaking. Above the main entrance a stone relief depicts the mighty scales of the cheesemakers' guild, and carved coats-of-arms embellish the façade on either side.

Turn left as you enter the ground floor to begin your tour of the museum by looking at the display on weighing-houses here and elsewhere in the Netherlands, where they were central to the communities they served and were often commissioned from leading architects as civic status symbols. Other displays on the ground floor, going round it clockwise, show the dairy process from grazing cow to finished product. More interesting – unless you are in the dairy business yourself or are accompanied by children with a school project in mind – are the displays on historic and contemporary Gouda. Cheese looms large here too; unless you are what might be called a tirophile, the top floor, with its exhibits on cheese consumption and cheese and the Dutch economy, can be skipped. If you're there on a Thursday in summer, when the cheeses are being weighed, you will not be allowed to leave without sampling a slice of freshly cut Gouda.

Facing the Waag across the square is the Stadhuis (Town Hall), at Markt no. 1. Built in 1450, it is the oldest free-standing Gothic town hall in the Netherlands. The ornate façade is decorated with carvings of the dukes and duchesses of Burgundy, whose lands stretched this far until the death of the last Duke, Charles the Bold (1433–1477), after which Gouda, like the rest of the Netherlands, became part of the Holy Roman Empire of the Hapsburgs. Within, the Town Hall is decorated with antique tapestries depicting hunting scenes and religious themes.

Churches and museums

From the Town Hall, walk south across the square to the Grote of Sint Janskerk (Great or St John's Church), an enormous pile which dominates a cluster of historic buildings by the Gouwe River. The late-Gothic basilica, with wooden vaulting, is the longest church in the Netherlands – 123m (403ft) in length – but is noted more for its seventy gorgeous stained-glass windows. Of these, some forty are survivors of the window-smashing, statue-breaking fury of the early Reformation, while the rest are post-Reformation additions. They show a variety of scenes from both the Old and New Testaments and also from local history. The window depicting Christ driving the money-changers from the temple was the gift of William the Silent. There are carillon concerts from the bell-tower on Thursday and Saturday mornings.

Now turn left, heading towards the Gouwe, which flows through the centre of town as a narrow canal. On your left, between the Sint Janskerk and the Catharina

Gasthuis, which will be your next stop, is a narrow, bell-gabled three-storey building with red and white shutters, the Lazaruspoortje (Lazarus Gate), leading into the court of the Gasthuis. The name recalls the Lazarus whom Christ raised from the dead, and also indicates the 14th-century building's role as a hospice for leprosy sufferers. The original building was expanded in the 17th century, with the addition of lavishly executed governor's rooms and a Classical façade. The museum has an excellent collection, spanning gruesome tools of torture and surgical instruments, 16th-century altarpieces, some fine paintings from the painters of the 19th-century Hague School and the French Barbizon painters, and glittering silver cups and plate, which belonged to the medieval guilds.

Leave the Catharina Gasthuis by the entrance facing the Gouwe. Cross to the Westhaven (the west bank of the Gouwe Canal) and, with the canal on your left, walk down to the Stedelijk Museum De Moriaan at no. 29 Westhaven.

The museum, in a 17th-century tobacco merchant's house and shop, is named Moriaan (Blackamoor) after the turbaned, pipe-smoking figure above the door. He brandishes a vast clay pipe in his right hand and a bundle of tobacco leaves in his left. The interior of the shop is intact and decorated with beautifully carved woodwork and marbled panels. The place has a vast collection of the clay pipes for which Gouda is famous.

Pipes and pottery

Walk on down the Westhaven for about 200m (220yd) until you reach the Kuiper-straat, running at right angles to the Gouwe, and turn right for one block to the corner of Peperstraat. Here, at no. 76, is the Adrie Moerings Goudse Pottebakkerij en Pijpenmakerij, one of several potteries in the city; you can watch clay pipes and pots being moulded and thrown by hand in the traditional way. The delicate long-stemmed pipes, decorated or in plain white pipeclay, make pretty souvenirs of the city, even for non-smokers. The pottery also makes and sells decorative ceramics in both the blue-and-white Delft style and the more richly coloured Gouda style.

Carry on down Peperstraat and take the next right. Follow this street as it curves left across the Bogen to the Vest, the canal waterfront on the west side of the inner city. On your left as you reach the water is the Binnenhaven Museum, on the former canal harbour, which has a collection of barges, engines and equipment.

Keeping the canal and its boats to your left, walk from this former boatyard to a prominent waterside landmark, the round brick tower of the Molen de Roode Leeuw (Red Lion Mill), at Vest no. 65. There has been a mill here since 1619, though there is no trace of the earliest wooden postmill. The present gallery-mill, built in 1727 and rebuilt in 1771, fell into disuse early this century. In 1926 it was bought by the municipality, but remained a virtual ruin until the 1980s, when renovation began. In February 1986, after a DFL 1.5 million restoration programme, the mill reopened as a functioning grain mill, and is the only working mill in the

Netherlands in which the miller still lives. Climb the tower for a good view over the centre of Gouda and its canals.

In 1850 there were around 10,000 windmills in the Netherlands. Only about 1000 survive as monuments to that era, before steam, diesel and electric power supplanted wind as the country's prime energy source. The Red Lion sells a variety of ground and milled grain to Gouda's bakeries and to wholefood stores and restaurants, and you yourself can buy some stone-ground flour or breakfast cereal to take home from the small shop downstairs. Other aspects of running the mill, like installing new sails, lifting bags of grain into the tower, and maintaining the grindstones, are all done in the traditional way.

Along the Gouwe

Turn your back on the canal and walk inland to the Raam, a main thoroughfare skirting the city-centre. Cross it, walk one block up, and turn left on Keizerstraat, which eventually curves around to the right to meet the Hoge Gouwe. Turn right along the canal, keeping it on your left. At nos. 39–41 Hoge Gouwe is the bulky Gouwe Kerk, a three-aisled neo-Gothic cross-basilica built in 1904 and conspicuously lacking the verve of the 15th-century Sint Janskerk. Walk past it and prepare to cross to the opposite bank. Either side of the bridge across the Gouwe are pillared galleries, built in the 17th century to shelter the city's korenbeurs (corn exchange) and vismarkt (fish market). Grain and fish were brought into the city by boat for auction to the city's merchants. The twin rivers were Gouda's highways and the main source of its early prosperity.

Turn left to cross the bridge and, at its end, turn left again, walking back along the opposite bank of the Gouwe, again keeping the canal on your left. Pass Achter de Vismarkt on your right, and turn left across the next bridge. Facing you at the other end of the bridge is the 17th-century clandestine Oud-Katholieke Kerk van St Hoannes de Doper (Old Catholic Church of St John the Baptist), a legacy of the period when Catholic worship was tolerated as long it was conducted discreetly behind closed doors.

Continue along the Hoge Gouwe, the canal now on your right, to the next bridge. Turn right to cross the canal and walk straight along the Turfmarkt (where boats brought loads of peat for the city's hearths) to no. 30, two blocks along. Here the Zuidhollands Verzetsmuseum (South Holland Resistance Museum) displays an impressive collection of pictures, makeshift weapons and documents such as forged passes and ration-books, marking the struggle of the local Resistance movement against German Occupation during World War II.

Walk on along the Turfmarkt to the Kleiweg, turn left, and retrace your steps to Stationsplein.

Utrecht

Utrecht likes to claim it is the oldest city in the Netherlands, tracing its descent from a Roman settlement established in AD48. More realistically, the earliest settlement can be dated from the eighth century, when Benedictine monks under the English Archbishop Willibrod (St Willibrod; c.658–739) established a foundation to bring Christianity to the then little-populated regions north of the Rhine. Until supplanted by newer settlements, Utrecht remained the most important city in the northern Low Countries. This walk takes you through its city-centre, visiting the cathedral and other historic buildings, and allows time to wander through Utrecht's choice of museums.

Start/finish: Stationsplein/Centraal Station; trains to and from Amsterdam Centraal Station about every 25 minutes; journey-time about 30 minutes

Length: 7km (4 1/2 miles)

Time: 4hr

Refreshments: Can be found throughout the walk – for winter days, there is a wide choice of sheltered cafés and restaurants in the Hoog Catharijne shopping mall, and on summer days the outdoor cafés along Oudegracht are recommended

To visit:
- Musical Clock and Organ Museum: Tuesday–Saturday 10.00–17.00, Sunday 13.00–17.00
- Domkerk/Domtoren: daily 09.00–17.00
- Centraal Museum: Tuesday–Saturday 11.00–17.00, Sunday 12.00–17.00
- Nederlands Spoorwegmuseum (railway museum): 10.00–17.00, Sunday 13.00–17.00
- Catharijneconvent Museum: Tuesday–Saturday 10.00–17.00, Sunday 13.00–17.00
- Pieterskerk: opening hours vary – enquire at Utrecht VV Tourist Information Office
- Museum voor het Krudeniersbedrijf (Grocery Museum): Tuesday–Saturday 10.00–17.00, Sunday 13.00–17.00

Walk across the Stationsplein and pass through the cavernous Hoog Catharijne shopping centre, a 24-hectare (58-acre) palace of consumerism with almost 200 shops, cafés and restaurants. Exiting the mall, walk straight on, keeping the car park on your left, and turn right into the Vredenburg just as it joins the Steenweg. The 112m (340ft) Domtoren (Cathedral Tower) is a prominent landmark ahead. Immediately after joining the Steenweg, turn right on the Donkerstraat. On the right is an imposing grey façade with red shutters, the 16th-century Zoudenbalch mansion,

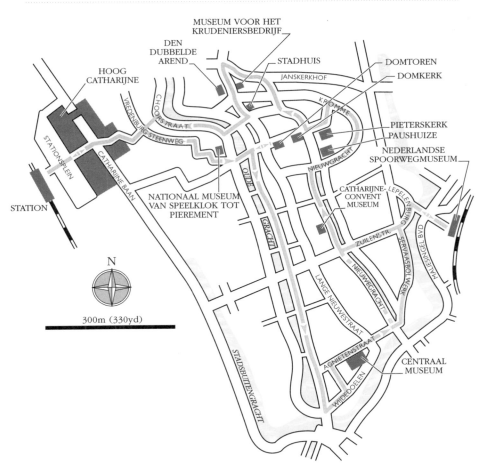

MUSEUM VOOR HET
KRUDENIERSBEDRIJF

DEN
DUBBELDE
AREND

STADHUIS

DOMTOREN
DOMKERK

HOOG
CATHARIJNE

JANSKERKHOF

KROMME

CHOORSTRAAT

VREEDENBURG STEENWEG

STATIONSPLEIN

CATHARIJNE BAAN

PIETERSKERK
PAUSHUIZE

NEDERLANDSE
SPOORWEGMUSEUM

NIEUWGRACHT

OUDE GRACHT

NATIONAAL MUSEUM
VAN SPEELKLOK TOT
PIEREMENT

STATION

CATHARIJNE-
CONVENT
MUSEUM

LEPELENBURG

ZUILENSTR.

SERVAASBOLWERK

MALIESINGEL BVD

N

NIEUWEGRACHT

300m (330yd)

LANGE NIEUWSTRAAT

STADSBUITENGRACHT

AGNIETENSTRAAT

WITTEVROUWEN

CENTRAAL
MUSEUM

home of a wealthy Utrecht family. Evert van Zoudenbalch, canon of the Domkerk, knocked the family's adjoining homes into one grand mansion and commissioned a solidly prosperous new front for it.

Opposite this prominent building, turn left into Derde (3e) Buurkerksteeg, a narrow lane which leads you to the Buurkerk. In medieval Utrecht, this was the church of the 'buurs' (commoners). High up on the façade, to your left, two cannonballs embedded in the wall are said to have been there since the bombardment of the city by the Spaniards in 1572.

The Buurkerk is now the Nationaal Museum 'Van Speelklok tot Pierement' (From Musical Clock to Barrel Organ), with a collection of automated musical instruments dating between the 18th century and the present day. The entrance is around the church to the right.

After visiting the museum, walk on towards the Domkerk, passing on your left the entrance to Choorstraat (Choir Street), so called because the choir of the Buurkerk stood here. Immediately in front of you is Oude Gracht, the canal which cuts the medieval city-centre in two, with the Maartensbrug (St Martin's Bridge) across it. Walk over this short bridge to the Domkerk, pausing to look at one of the decorative canal lanterns of Oude Gracht. Each tells some local legend; this one depicts Sister Bertken, a 15th-century nun who locked herself away from the world for sixty years in a cell beneath the Buurkerk.

Tower and cathedral

Just before reaching the Domtoren, on your right at the opposite end of the short Servetstraat, is a tiny medieval house, all that remains of the palace of the Bishop of Utrecht. Next to it is an arched gateway bearing the date 1634. This is the entrance to Flora's Hof, a small herb-garden which once belonged to the palace. Triangular stone plaques on the back wall show scenes from the life of St Martin, Utrecht's patron saint. Leave this peaceful courtyard by the lane running to the right of the gateway and leading to Domplein (if the garden is closed, walk straight on into Domplein and around the tower to the entrance).

You now enter the 14th-century Domtoren, at 112m (367ft) the highest church tower in the Netherlands, and ascend its 465 breathtaking steps to the highest gallery for an equally breathtaking view.

Pause for breath 50m (165ft) above ground-level in the belfry. With its thirteen bells — weighing a total of thirty-four tons — the carillon here has the widest range in Europe. The bells play a different tune at each quarter-hour. The topmost tier of the three-tiered tower — built between 1321 and 1382 — is an eight-sided stone lantern.

Cross the Domplein to the Domkerk, whose soaring Gothic spires and flying buttresses dominate this side of the square. Midway between the cathedral and the tower stands a statue of John, Count of Nassau, brother of William the Silent.

Like so many of Europe's great cathedrals, the Domkerk took generations to build. It was begun in 1254, to replace an earlier Romanesque cathedral burned in the great fire which in 1253 devastated the city, and was completed in 1520, just in time for the early stirrings of the Reformation, which swept away the elaborate religious decorations of its Catholic interior to replace them with the plain whitewash and simple furnishings of the Calvinist faith.

The nave of the church, which was built to connect it with the Domtoren, fell in during the course of a terrible storm in 1674, creating the open space which is now the Domplein.

A cross of churches

The church was built at the centre of what is known as Utrecht's 'cross of churches'; it is surrounded by the Janskerk, Pieterskerk, Mariakerk and the Abbey of St Paul.

Turn back into the square, retrace your steps past the Domtoren, and turn right along the length of Oude Gracht, known as the 'sunken canal': its waterside terraces, unusually for a Dutch city canal, are some 1.5m (4ft) below street-level in the city-centre. Keeping the canal to your right, walk all the way down to its junction with Stadsbuitengracht, the canal that rings the city-centre and which originally formed a moat beyond the city walls. Turn left onto Wijdedoelen and walk parallel to Stadsbuitengracht, with the canal-side park on your right. Take the second left and walk up Nicolaasdwarsstraat to the Nicolaaskerk; then turn right onto Agnietenstraat. The Centraal Museum, at no. 1, is on your right.

Dolls and Vikings

The museum is all about Utrecht, and has some fine paintings in addition to more obscure exhibits. High-points include a reconstructed Viking ship, dating from around AD1200. Viking raiders from Denmark, Scotland and northern England harried the towns and monasteries of the Low Countries for some four centuries. Look out for the delightful 17th-century dolls' house, next to the costume gallery to the right of the entrance. Wonderful craftsmanship went into the making of this three-storey house, its family of 23cm (9in) residents and their servants, and their possessions. On the mezzanine floor there is a room devoted to the works of Jan van Scorel, the Utrecht painter and inventor sometimes called the 'Dutch Leonardo'; next door a clutch of more modern painters, including Van Gogh and Mondrian, are exhibited.

Leaving the museum, turn right and walk to the end of Agnietenstraat. Railway enthusiasts should now cross Nieuwegracht and follow the Servaasbolwerk – as the name implies, once a bulwark of the city wall – through the canal-side park to the canal bridge at the corner of Lepelenburg. Cross the canal and the Maliesingel Boulevard and walk up Jan van Oldenbarneveldlaan to the Nederlandse Spoorweg-museum (Netherlands Railway Museum).

Full steam ahead

The Railway Museum is housed in the antique Maliebaan Station, and is a rail enthusiast's treasury, with more than 60 locomotives, carriages and freight wagons. Inside, moving models, paintings and films tell the story of railways in the Netherlands.

Retrace your steps across the canal, return to the junction of Lepelenburg and Servaasbolwerk, and walk straight ahead along Schalkwijkstaat to Nieuwegracht. Cross the canal, and in front of you is the Catharijnecovent Museum.

The museum, adjoining the 15th-century St Catharijnekerk – now a Catholic cathedral church – is dedicated to the history of Christianity in the Netherlands, and boasts the largest collection of medieval art in the country.

Start by visiting the basement, where a collection of gorgeous church vestments from as early as the 14th century is displayed. On the next floor is a collection of religious art, including works by van Scorel and the Leiden painter Geertgen tot Sint Jans, while upstairs are more portraits and interiors by Pieter Saenredam, Rembrandt, Frans Hals and other painters.

Return to Nieuwegracht and turn left, following the canal until it curves sharply right. Cross the canal into Pausdam and turn right to follow Nieuwegracht. On your left is the Paushuize, a step-gabled 16th-century mansion built as the residence of Pope Adrian VI, born Adriaan Floriszoon Boeyens (1459–1523) in Utrecht. He was elected pope in 1522 but died after only a year in office, without ever visiting the house his proud fellow citizens had built for him. It is now used by the Utrecht provincial council.

Utrecht's oldest church

Continue around the loop of Nieuwegracht and, shortly after the place where it changes its name to become the Kromme, turn left into the Pieterskerkhof. The 11th-century Romanesque Pieterskerk is the earliest in Utrecht and perhaps the oldest in the Netherlands; it was consecrated in 1048. Red-sandstone pillars support the nave, and in the choir are two 12th-century reliefs, one showing Pilate, the other showing the Crucifixion and the empty tomb. In the crypt is the tomb of Bishop Bernold, who commissioned the church and died six years after its completion. He was one of a line of bishops of Utrecht who, in their 11th- and 12th-century heyday, were the most powerful feudal rulers in the Netherlands, commanding the fealty of the counts of Holland and other, lesser nobles.

Grocers and bakers

Walk to the end of Pieterskerkhof, turn right into Achter Sint Piter; then, at the junction of Oudkerkhof and Domstraat, turn right again and follow the Korte Jansstraat until you reach its junction with Janskerkhof. Here you will find the Janskerk facing you on the opposite side of the road. Look at the small figure of Anne Frank by Pieter d'Hont, then turn left and left again into the Teilingstraat. Yet another left takes you into a small dead-end street, the Hoogt, and here, at no. 6, is the Museum voor het Krudeniersbedrijf (Grocery Museum), a well kept traditional shop with old-fashioned counter, scales, fittings and cash-box, plus barrels and jars of goods.

Retracing your steps, turn left into the Teilingstraat, walk on into Scoutenstraat, and your nose will lead you to the source of the smell of fresh baking: no. 13. Den Dubbelde Arend, Utrecht's oldest bakery, was built in the first half of the 16th century, and its old ovens and shop interior are preserved working and intact. From the bakery, walk past the Stadhuis (on your left), turn right on Oudkerkhof, cross the canal and turn right along Choorstraat. At Drie Haringstraat, the fifth on your left, turn left to return to the Hoog Catharijne and the railway station.

Leiden 1: Young Rembrandt

Rembrandt made his career in Amsterdam. Most visitors to the Netherlands associate him with the country's best-known city, but he was born in Leiden, and lived here until he was 26. It was here that he studied the Classical writers, became fascinated with the stories of the Old Testament and the myths of Classical Greece and Ancient Rome, decided to become a painter and – after an apprenticeship in Leiden and Amsterdam – first established himself as a freelance artist. Many of his earliest masterpieces were created in his Leiden studio. This walk takes you in his early footsteps.

Start/finish:	Stationsplein; trains every 30 minutes to and from Amsterdam Centraal Station; journey-time about 40 minutes
Length:	6.4km (4 miles)
Time:	$2\,^1/_2$ hr
Refreshments:	Cafés and restaurants in the Pieterskerkplein and surrounding streets
Which day:	Any day
To visit:	● Pieterskerk: Monday–Saturday 09.00–17.00
	● The Burcht: Monday–Saturday 09.00–17.00

Leave the station by Stationsweg, cross the Morssingel Canal on the outskirts of the city and enter the Steenstraat on the opposite bank. Follow this road to the corner of Morsstraat and continue with the water of the Rijn (Rhine) river on your left. The river bank takes a sharp right turn; and now you find yourself on the Kort Galgewater, Leiden's historic river harbour. Follow it past the corner of the Smidsteeg. On the waterfront is a solid red-brick building with a tall step-gable facing the water. This was the Stadstimmerwerf (Town Carpenters' Wharf) workshop, and is now a sheltered housing complex for elderly people. Rembrandt lived immediately opposite, on the other side of the Galgewater Canal. The reconstruction of his studio in the former painter's workshop at Kort Galgewater no. 24A is used by Leiden painter Jacob Kanbier, who paints and exhibits his work in the studio; you can look over his shoulder while he paints, or even take a hands-on lesson in painting.

Windmills

Walk on along the Kort Galgewater to the place where three waterways meet; here there is a swing bridge across the mouth of the Galgewater. Before turning left to cross this, stop at the De Put Windmill, an unmissable waterside landmark. The windmill which currently stands on the site was built in 1987 and is an authentic reconstruction of the mill which stood here in 1669. That original windmill was built in 1619 by Jan Janszoon Put, after the Leiden council granted him permission to move it from a site east of the town. (Windmills – like some other farm buildings –

could quite easily be dismantled and rebuilt elsewhere. The tower might be made of wood or stone, and the machinery was made almost entirely of wood, except for the grindstones.) The location, exposed to the west wind, was ideal, and we can be sure that the 13-year-old Rembrandt must have watched the reassembly of the mill with great interest.

From the gateway to the windmill, retrace your steps to the mouth of the Galgewater and cross the Rembrandtbrug (Rembrandt Bridge). Your view down the Rijn to your right is partly blocked by the modern railway bridge; just on the other side of it, on the right bank of the river, Rembrandt's grandfather Gerrit Roelofszoon had a windmill. It was fired by Spanish besiegers in 1573 in their efforts to starve Leiden's defenders into submission. They failed, and the forces of William of Orange finally liberated the city on 3 October 1574, an event which is still celebrated to this day in a lively annual festival.

The bridge leads you into Weddesteeg, where Rembrandt's family had lived for at least two generations – his grandfather, aunt and great-aunt all had homes here – before his birth on 15 July 1606; he lived here until 1631. His grandparents built a windmill here atop the double town wall which then ran along the right-hand side of the Weddesteeg, to replace the one they had lost to the Spaniards; by 1575 they had sold it and bought yet another.

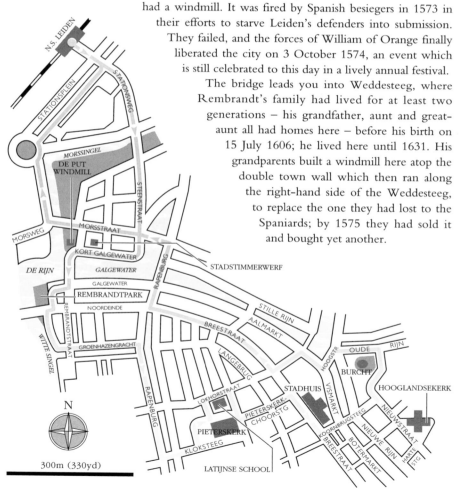

Sadly, Rembrandt's birthplace was demolished at the beginning of the 20th century, and now the only trace which remains of the family home is a stone plaque erected in 1906.

Turn right almost immediately at the end of the bridge and walk through the Schildersplaats, turning left along the side of the Rembrandtpark, a small patch of greenery at the water's edge. Opposite you, across the Noordeinde, where the Boerhaave School now stands, Rembrandt's brother owned a windmill. In Rembrandt's day, the waterside of the Witte Singel around here was a patchwork of small kitchen gardens; in 1630 Rembrandt himself bought a section of canal-side land at a price of 500 guilders to use as a garden.

Conscription
Cross the Noordeinde and go through the subway below the Boerhaave School. Reaching the bank of the Witte Singel, walk along it with the canal on your right. Opposite, on the corner of the Witte Singel, is Leiden's only memorial statue of Rembrandt, a bust sculpted in 1906 by Toon Dupui. At the corner of Groenhazen-gracht, turn left and walk past the end of the undistinguished Rembrandtstraat (named after the painter in 1879). Further along, the Oude Varkenmarkt (Old Pigmarket) on your left must have been a noisy, smelly part of town in Rembrandt's day, and best avoided unless you had pressing business there. On the other side of this street is the Doelenpoort.

The gate was built in 1645; a relief depicts St Joris (St George), patron saint of the Leiden militia, in battle with the dragon. The part of town called the Doelen, now the site of Leiden University, was the training-ground and firing range for the Leiden Civic Guard companies. The citizen guards were responsible for defending the town against outside attack, and they also provided a reserve of trained troops for the regular army in times of war, while in times of peace they acted as a police force, patrolling the streets at night.

Each healthy male citizen between the ages of 18 and 60 was obliged to serve in the guard, provided he could afford to buy his own equipment. Millers, like Rembrandt's father Harmen, hated night-watch duty as it meant they had to close down the mill. Rembrandt's father was injured when his musket exploded in his hands; after the wounds healed, he bought himself out of night-patrol duty for six guilders a year, and in 1617, when one of Rembrandt's brothers joined the guard to take his place, Harmen was discharged altogether.

Education and religion
At the end of Groenhazengracht turn right along the Rapenburg, keeping the canal on your left. In the early 17th century this was a quiet canal on the outskirts of the city, but in Rembrandt's lifetime it became one of the most prestigious canals in Leiden, attracting the city's wealthiest families.

At no. 73 Rapenburg you come to the site of the Academiegebouw (University Senate Building), the principal seat of the University of Leiden since 1581. In 1620, Rembrandt was registered as a student at the university at the early age of 14; most students entered the university when they were 17 or 18. The exception made for Rembrandt may have been because the headmaster of the Latijnse School, where he was a pupil, recognized him as a particularly bright student. In any case, Rembrandt had already decided to be a painter. He did not complete his grammar-school education, and never actually attended the university.

Now turn left across the Nonnenbrug and walk along the Kloksteeg as far as the Pieterskerkplein. The entrance to the Pieterskerk (St Peter's Church) is on the north side of the square. Rembrandt's family worshipped here and – like other Leiden folk – passed through the church on weekdays too, using it as a shortcut between the Herensteeg on one side and the Pieterkerkstraat on the other. The church was also a centre of community entertainment, with music on the church organ almost every evening. Many Leiden families had burial vaults in the church; the Rembrandt family vault was in front of the pulpit, and both Rembrandt's parents and many of his brothers and sisters are buried here, though Rembrandt himself was buried at the Westerkerk in Amsterdam (see page 43).

During the 19th century the interior of the church was rearranged and the graves surrounding the pulpit were moved. The Rembrandt family stone is probably one of three now nameless stones in front of the pulpit.

Leaving the Pieterskerk, cross diagonally to your left and enter the Muskadelsteeg. At the end of this narrow lane, on your right at Lokhorstraat no. 16, is the Latijnse School. This was where the children of well-to-do Leiden families were sent as pupils, and it was here that Rembrandt learnt Latin and Greek, penmanship, verse and music. As the youngest son of an affluent miller, he had good prospects; while his elder brothers could expect to inherit shares in the family mills, he might have become a minister – then a position of high standing in Dutch society – or a doctor. His schooling certainly gave him a grounding in the Classics and in the Old Testament, providing many of the mythological and biblical themes which later fascinated him.

Turn right into the Lokhorstraat and right again into the Pieterkerkstraat, then left into Pieterskerkchoorsteeg and across the Langebrug.

Jacob Swanenburg (1571–1638), Rembrandt's first tutor in drawing and painting, lived at no. 89 Langebrug. The young Rembrandt was apprenticed for three years to Swanenburg, who had studied in Italy and whose works were on familiar religious themes such as Hell and damnation; Swanenburg's fondness for stereotyped canvases of sinners, devils and dragons hardly appears to have rubbed off on his pupil. Later, Rembrandt studied under Pieter Lastman in Amsterdam for six months. He was clearly a fast study, because at the end of this period he was able to return to Leiden and begin making a living as a painter.

Buying and selling

Pieterskerkchoorsteeg leads into the Breestraat, where you can see the façade of Leiden's Stadhuis (Town Hall) right in front of you. In Rembrandt's time, the Town Hall was far more than just the seat of local government: it was a focus for all sorts of community activities. The patrols of the night watch gathered here at dusk before setting out to police the city. Meat and poultry were sold from stalls in front of the building, and the streets around it were full of shops and stalls trading in goods and farm produce. The Stadhuis came into its own during the annual fairs – a favourite subject for contemporary painters – when the great hall at the top of the stairs was used for the sale of paintings. This annual event offered the burghers of Leiden the chance to buy the works of painters from all over the Netherlands, and was not entirely welcomed by the local artists. Rembrandt's contemporary Jan Lievens – another pupil of Lastman's – tried to limit competition from outside town by establishing a fixed day for the sale of paintings, but imports continued to threaten the comfortable monopoly of the Leiden painters.

Walk along the Breestraat the length of the Town Hall and turn left into Koornbrugsteeg (Corn Bridge Alley) and the Stadhuisplein. Before the great fire of 1929 ravaged the Town Hall and the nearby streets, a row of medieval shops stood along the Vismarkt (Fishmarket) waterfront, overlooking the channel of the Nieuwe Rijn (New Rhine). Several of Rembrandt's family had businesses or homes here. Around 1600 the painter's great-grandmother lived at a house called The Golden Pig – houses at the time had evocative names instead of street numbers. The house next door was a bakery run by his mother's father.

No. 43 Nieuwe Rijn, beside the canal, was the home of a scholar named Petrus Scriverius, who may have been one of Rembrandt's early patrons – 'two great masterpieces by Rembrandt' were listed as part of the estate of Scriverius' eldest son in 1663. The Koornbeursbrug, crossing the Nieuwe Rijn, served a dual purpose, being not just a bridge: beneath covered arcades on either side of the roadway was the Leiden grain market. Cross the bridge and turn right, walking along the Nieuwe Rijn with the water on your right. The opposite bank, the Botermarkt, was the medieval dairy-market street.

Relatives and contemporaries

Turn left into Hartesteeg and left again at the corner of Nieuwstraat, walking past the Hooglandsekerk (or Pancraskerk) on your right, and go through the gateway at the end of the street into the Burchtplein. In front of you is a squat brick fortress, the Burcht, built as early as the 11th century to protect the villagers of Leiden and the surrounding farms from floods and marauders. Climb to the battlements for a fine view of the surrounding countryside and the city.

Walk rightwards around the Burcht to the Oude Rijn, turn left, and, keeping the river to your right, walk to its junction with the Nieuwe Rijn at Hoogstraat.

Rembrandt's brother Willem lived at no. 7. Willem was a miller but – like Rembrandt himself – appears to have had a poor head for money, falling deeper and deeper into debt and being eventually driven to plead for work as a municipal grain-porter. Like his brother, he too was eventually forced to sell his house to pay his debts. He died of the plague in 1655.

Go on along Hoogstraat and, at its south end, walk across the Visbrug, Leiden's oldest bridge, past the Waagebouw (the municipal weigh-house) – on your right at the corner of Aalmarkt – to enter the Maarsmansteeg. Rembrandt's family lawyer lived at no. 21. A pharmacist called Christiaen Poret, who lived in this street in Rembrandt's time, was known for his collection of curios from all over the known world – an emu's egg, an ivory globe, mummified limbs, oriental scrolls, stones claimed to have magical healing powers . . .

Turn right at the end of the Maarsmansteeg and walk along the Breestraat, passing the Waalse Kerk (Walloon Church) and the Stadsgehoozal (Town Auditorium). Both buildings were originally part of a monastery hospice, the Catharinagasthuis. It had its own brewery, and Rembrandt's great-great-grandfather is recorded as having supplied the brewers with ground malt in 1484. The family mill was still supplying the brewery in Rembrandt's lifetime.

At the end of Breestraat, turn right into Kort Rapenburg, where the painter Gerard (Gerrit) Dou (1613–1675) was born at no. 9. Dou was first apprenticed to his father, a stained-glass artist, and became skilled in this art before being apprenticed to Rembrandt. He was an apt pupil, going on to found what is now called the Leiden School, characterized by the delicate brushwork of Dou and his imitators. They specialized in finely detailed interior scenes and obscure, punning allusions.

Cross the Rijn to Prinsessekade, where a madhouse and plague-house stood in Rembrandt's day, and turn left across the Blauwpoortsbrug to Morsstraat. Follow this street to the Morspoort (Mors Gate), a substantial brick gateway piercing a remnant of the 17th-century city wall. The Morspoort was built in 1668 to replace the earlier wooden Galgepoort (Gallows Gate); the city gallows stood on the Morsweg, on the other side of the Morssingel. In an early example of civic public relations, Leiden's city council decided the original name was infelicitous, and the new gate got a new name.

From the gateway, cross the short bridge across the Morssingel canal and turn right on Morsweg to return to Stationsplein.

Leiden 2: City almshouses

Almshouses (hofjes), run by charitable foundations to accommodate the elderly poor, have been a feature of life in Dutch towns since medieval times. Leiden has 35 of these idyllic courtyards, hidden away from the bustle of the streets. Many are architectural gems with rich historic associations. This walk takes you through a selection of them. Almshouse residents do not object to your visiting their pretty courtyards, but visitors are asked to take the residents' need for peace and privacy into consideration.

Start/finish:	Stationsplein; trains every 30 minutes to and from Amsterdam Centraal Station; journey-time about 40 minutes
Length:	6.4km (4 miles)
Time:	2–3hr
Refreshments:	Cafés and taverns around the Pieterskerkplein
Which day:	Any day
To visit:	• Hortus Botanicus (Botanical Gardens): Monday–Saturday 09.00–17.00, Sunday and holidays 10.00–17.00
	• Leidse Pilgrim Collectie (Leiden Pilgrim Collection): Monday–Friday 09.30–16.30

Leave Stationsplein by Stationsweg, cross the Morssingel, and walk down Steenstraat. On your right, at no. 17 Steenstraat, are the St Salvator almshouses. The Dutch word 'hof' means 'court' or 'courtyard'; the traditional almshouse is built around a communal inner garden, usually with only one doorway onto the street. A caretaker was responsible for opening and closing the gates at fixed times. Almshouses were usually founded by the wealthy, and the residents were charged with praying for the souls of their benefactors. Sometimes the founders began building during their own lifetimes; more usually, they left instructions to their heirs.

The St Salvator hofje was founded by Paulus de Goede, a Catholic priest from a wealthy Leiden family which rejected the Protestant doctrine of the Reformation. The building was completed in 1639 and was restored in 1991. Look out for the pointed arches above the windows, which are a rarity in Dutch architecture. Like most post-Reformation almshouse courts, this one has twelve individual houses. Before the Reformation the usual number was thirteen, perhaps in memory of Jesus and his twelve apostles; after the Reformation this may, perhaps, have been thought blasphemous.

Walk on down the Steenstraat to its end at Blauwpoortsbrug (Blue Gate Bridge), on your left. Until 1611, the Blue Gate was one of the gateways through the city wall. As the city grew, however, a new ring of fortifications was added along the line of the Morssingel, where the Mors Gate (see page 140) now stands. Turn left across the bridge, then right into Prinsessekade and across the Nieuwe Rijn Canal into Kort

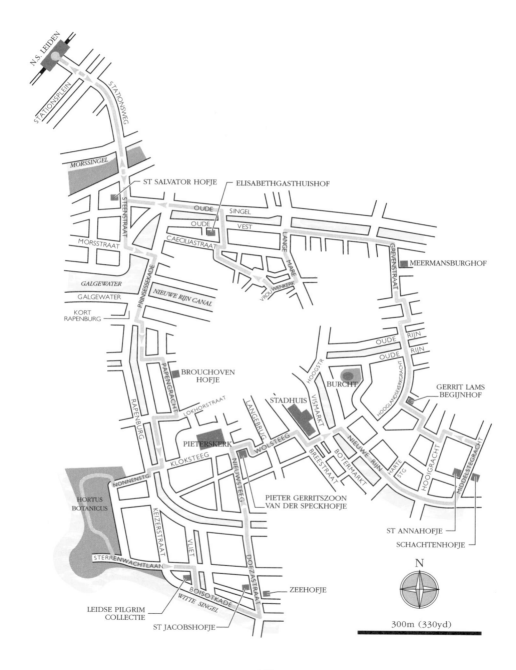

N.S. LEIDEN

STATIONSPLEIN

STATIONSWEG

MORSSINGEL

ST SALVATOR HOFJE

ELISABETHGASTHUISHOF

STEENSTRAAT

OUDE SINGEL

OUDE VEST

CAECILIASTRAAT

MORSSTRAAT

LANGE MARE

GREVENSTRAAT

MEERMANSBURGHOF

GALGEWATER

GALGEWATER

PRINSESSEKADE

NIEUWE RIJN CANAL

VROUWENKERK

KORT RAPENBURG

OUDE RIJN

OUDE RIJN

PAPENGRACHT

BROUCHOVEN HOFJE

HOOGSTR

HOOGLANDSEKERKGRACHT

RAPENBURG

LOKHORSTRAAT

LANGEBRUG

STADHUIS

VISMARKT

BURCHT

GERRIT LAMS BEGIJNHOF

PIETERSKERK

WOLSTEEG

NIEUWE RIJN

HARTE STG

HOOIGRACHT

MIDDELSTEEGRACHT

KLOKSTEEG

BREESTRAAT

BOTERMARKT

NONNENSTG.

NIEUWSTEEG

KEIZERSTRAAT

HORTUS BOTANICUS

PIETER GERRITSZOON VAN DER SPECKHOFJE

ST ANNAHOFJE

SCHACHTENHOFJE

VLIET

STERRENWACHTLAAN

DOEZASTRAAT

BOISOTKADE

WITTE SINGEL

ZEEHOFJE

N

LEIDSE PILGRIM COLLECTIE

ST JACOBSHOFJE

300m (330yd)

Rapenburg. With the canal on your right, walk down to the Langebrug and turn left, then right into Papengracht. Here, at no. 16, are the Brouchoven almshouses, built by Jacob van Brouchoven at the urging of his sister Anna. Anna left two existing houses to the foundation, and in 1640, towards the end of his own life, Jacob added twelve more one-storey cottages; the second storeys were added later in the 18th century. The little gatehouse bears the date 1640 and Jacob's and Anna's initials. On his death in 1642 Jacob handed over the almshouses to the municipality.

What was life like in these little institutions? That depended very much on the governing body. The governors were usually relatives of the founder and could rule over virtually all aspects of the resident's life. Residents were expected to show every sign of gratitude and respect for their great good fortune in finding free accommodation and other benefits – bread, meat, beer, shirts and shoes. Since the alternative was to starve in the street, they were probably punctilious in showing their appreciation. Almshouse life was usually a model of peace and rectitude.

The Botanical Gardens and the Pilgrim Collection

Carry on in the same direction down Papengracht to the Houtstraat and turn right, heading back towards the Rapenburg. Turn left along the canal, keeping it once again on your right.

On the other side of the canal is the Academiegebouw (University Senate). Originally a convent of the Dominican or White Nuns, it was taken over by the newly established university in 1581. Carry on along the Rapenburg until you reach the corner of Kloksteeg. Turn right here to cross the canal, and walk along Nonnensteeg to the Hortus Botanicus (Botanical Gardens).

The Hortus, close to the four-century-old university, has been Leiden's study garden since 1590, and is one of Europe's oldest botanical gardens. Within it, the Clusius Garden is a true copy of the original garden. Other high points include fine rose gardens, steamy greenhouses full of exotic orchids, giant lily-pads and a 350-year-old laburnum, the oldest tree in the Hortus. Enjoy wandering here on the banks of the Witte Singel before you leave via Sterrenwachtlaan.

Walk past the crossing with Keizerstraat and turn right on the Vliet, a short canal which seems to come to a dead end ahead of you at a high arched bridge, the Vlietbrug. Built in 1610, this is the oldest original bridge in Leiden (others, like the Rembrandtbrug, are reconstructions of earlier bridges).

At no. 45 Vliet is the Leiden Pilgrim Collection, a small museum dedicated to the English Puritans who settled in Leiden in the early 17th century before setting out in 1620 to found their colony in America. A narrow lane leads out of the small square on your left – the Ruime Consientieplein – to the Boisotkade, which overlooks the waters of the Witte Singel, Leiden's outer canal ring. Turn left along the canal and left again onto Doezastraat, where at no. 25 stands the entrance of the St Jacobshofje, or Crayenbosch almshouse, founded by Gomarus Jacobszoon van Crayenbosch, a rich

Catholic merchant who lived on Hooigracht and had this hofje built, according to his will, after his death in 1672. This is one of the smaller almshouse-courts, with only nine houses – indeed, it had only six houses at first because, by the time van Crayenbosch left his bequest, building space was at a premium within the Leiden city limits. Three more houses were added in 1883, and the courtyard was restored in 1977.

Family matters

Opposite is another hofje, founded by Samuel de Zee. The inscriptions above the inner and outer entrances indicate that the founder, who died childless, left his money to the poor to spite his greedy nephews and nieces, who had anticipated inheriting his wealth. The message above the street door translates as: 'For good, but not rich, nieces and nephews.' Samuel began building during his lifetime, and in 1743 eleven more houses and a governors' room were added. The governors' room of an almshouse was the meeting place of the governing body, and was often extremely richly furnished, in contrast with the adequate but plain accommodation afforded the residents.

Continue up the Doezastraat, which leads you back to the Rapenburg, which you cross. Ahead of you is the unmissable landmark of the Pieterskerk. Keep going along what is now called Nieuwsteeg, and then detour left into Kloksteeg.

Jean Pesijn, who built the almshouse at no. 21, was a Protestant fugitive from near Lille in northern France. He and his wife, Marie de Lannoy, founded it in memory of their only daughter, who had died during the plague of 1655. The hofje is located in what is still called the 'English Passage', a narrow close leading off the Kloksteeg and built by the English followers of the Puritan divine John Robinson (*c*.1576–1625), who had fled to Protestant Leiden as a result of religious persecution at home. In search of even greater freedom to follow their beliefs, many of them ultimately abandoned Leiden for the New World, setting sail from Plymouth in the *Mayflower* in 1620. Robinson, however, was not among these Pilgrim Fathers. He remained in Leiden until his death, and is buried in the Pieterskerk.

A wealthy carpenter and a rich brewer

Retrace your steps along the south side of the church and you will find yet another almshouse-courtyard, the Pieter Gerritszoon van der Speckhofje, half-hidden behind a huge chestnut tree on your right at the corner of Kloksteeg and Nieuwesteeg.

Pieter Speck – sometimes called van der Speck (perhaps he liked to give himself airs) – was a wealthy carpenter who owned many houses in Leiden. He built the hofje himself, close to his own home, but was able to squeeze only eight houses into the space available. His will in 1645 laid down the rules of the foundation and left funds for its upkeep.

Unlike many hofjes, the Speck courtyard has more than one entrance. Pass through the inner court to emerge in a larger courtyard, then turn left through a large gateway that brings you to the Langebrug. Cross this, and walk along the Wolsteeg, at the end of which turn right, then left around the Town Hall onto the Koornbrugsteeg. Cross the bridge and walk right along the ring of the Nieuwe Rijn. After four blocks, turn left, away from the canal, up Middelstegracht, where you will find the St Annahofje about 50m (55yd) along on your left.

Willem Claeszoon, a rich brewer, endowed this almshouse on his death in 1491. His children built homes for thirteen elderly women and provided them with their own chapel, arousing the professional jealousy of the priest of the nearby Hooglandsekerk. He feared a rival place of worship would lure away his congregation, and after much wrangling it was agreed that only the old ladies of the hofje might attend mass in the chapel there. Tucked away within an inner courtyard, the chapel is one of only a few to have survived the ravages of the Reformation more or less intact.

More almshouses

On the opposite side of the street, at no. 27, is the Schachtenhofje, one of Leiden's more striking hofjes, with a façade designed by the city's master carpenter, Willem van der Helm, in 1671. Anthonis van der Schacht, the founder, came to prosperity making lace and ribbons, but had grown up in poverty in an orphanage. He died during the great plague of 1669–70, leaving five houses on Middelstegracht to be converted into almshouses. Look for the letters 'R' and 'P' engraved on the twin spouts of the water-pump in the courtyard; rainwater (R) came out of one, pump-water (P) out of the other.

A series of zigzags follows: take the next left into the Kloosterpoort, follow it to the corner of Hooigracht, turn left, then cross the street and take the first right into Hooglandsekerkchoorsteeg. Follow this narrow street to the Hooglandskerk, turn right along the Middenweg, then first left and walk along the Moriaansteeg to Hooglandsekerkgracht. On the right, at no. 38, are the Mierennest almshouses. Their name means 'anthill', and indicates that this must have been a teeming urban slum at the time the Gerrit Lams Begijnhof, one of Leiden's oldest almshouses, was built in the 15th century. Originally a beguinage – a community of lay nuns – the property came under the control of the Protestant Church after the Reformation and was used to house the poor. In 1731 the houses were bought by Diederick van Leyden, a churchwarden, and in his will he provided for them to be transformed into proper almshouses. The buildings were extensively restored in 1982.

Walk along Hooglandsekerkgracht to its end, cross the Oude Rijn (Old Rhine) and Haarlemmerstraat, and, doing a quick right–left, walk up the Lombardsteeg, across the Van der Werfstraat for a quick left–right into Grevenstraat. Follow this street up to the waters of the Oude Singel and the Oude Vest. At no. 159 is the grandest of Leiden's almshouses, the Meermansburghof.

In 1596 the derelict Nazarether Cloister on this site was replaced by a block of sixty-three small homes for labourers. These lasted less than a century, and were demolished by the wealthy Maerten Meerman to make way for his almshouses in 1680. The court was rebuilt again in 1778–80, when a magnificent stucco ceiling was added to the governors' room. The pump in the inner court is crowned by a castle and a merman – one of those visual puns on the family name which so delighted Dutch builders.

Leaving the Meermansburg, turn left along the canal at Oude Vest and follow it to the second bridge; ignoring the bridge, turn left into Lange Mare. Just beyond the bridge is the Marekerk, built in 1638–48. Walk down Lange Mare and take the third turning on the right, the Vrouwenkerkkoortsteeg, walking rightwards into the Vrouwenkerksplein. The foundations of the old church can still be seen in the square as you walk across it, bearing right.

Bypassing the entrance to Vrouwenkerksteeg on your left, take the next turning left and walk along to the corner of Sionsteeg, where your landmark is the gateway to the Sionshofje, built in 1668. Turn right here, then almost immediately left into a small square, on which stands the last almshouse-courtyard on this walk, the Elisabethgasthuishof, a foundation originally attached to the Sint Elisabeth City Hospital.

Lange Lijsbethsteeg, on the right, takes you back to the Oude Singel. Cross it by the footbridge, turn left on Oude Singel and walk straight on, crossing the Nieuwe Beestemarkt, to Steenstraat, where you turn right to return to Stationsplein.

Leiden 3: Museums

*Leiden, the oldest university city in the Netherlands, has been a centre of learning
for more than four centuries and has more than its fair share of museums. This walk
takes you to a collection of archaeological finds from all over the world, a seven-storey
windmill museum, a collection of minor masterpieces by Rembrandt and his contemporaries,
and a selection of other weird and wonderful exhibitions. This is a good walk for a wet or
cold and wintry day, with plenty of indoor attractions not too far apart.*

Start/finish: Stationsplein; trains every 30 minutes to and from Amsterdam
Centraal Station; journey-time about 40 minutes
Length: 5km (3 miles)
Time: $2^{1}/_{2}$ hr
Refreshments: Lots of cafés and taverns along Houtstraat, or detour to the
Pieterskerkhof for more of the same
Which day: Not Mondays
To visit:
- Rijksmuseum voor Volkenkunde (National Museum of
Ethnology): Tuesday–Friday 10.00–17.00, Saturday–Sunday
12.00–17.00
- Wagenmakersmuseum (Cartwrights' Museum):
Tuesday–Saturday 10.00–17.00, Sunday 12.00–17.00
- Academisch Historisch Museum (Museum of University
History): Wednesday–Friday 13.00–17.00
- Rijksmuseum van Oudenheden (National Museum of
Antiquities): Tuesday–Saturday 10.00–17.00, Sundays and
holidays 12.00–17.00
- Rijksmuseum het Koninklijk Penningkabinet (National
Museum of the Royal Coin Cabinet): Tuesday–Saturday
10.00–17.00, Sundays and holidays 12.00–17.00
- Gemeentearchief (City Archive): Monday–Friday 09.30–17.00,
Saturday 09.00–12.15
- Boerhaave Museum: Tuesday–Saturday 10.00–17.00,
Sunday 12.00–17.00
- Stedelijk Museum de Lakenhal: Tuesday–Friday 10.00–17.00,
weekends and holidays 12.00–17.00
- Molen De Valk (Falcon Windmill): Tuesday–Saturday
10.00–17.00, Sundays and holidays 13.00–17.00

Leave Stationsplein by Stationsweg, turning right – away from the station and
towards the town-centre. Cross the Morssingel and turn right into the Mors Singel
Park just before you reach the 1e/2e Binnenvestgracht crossroad.

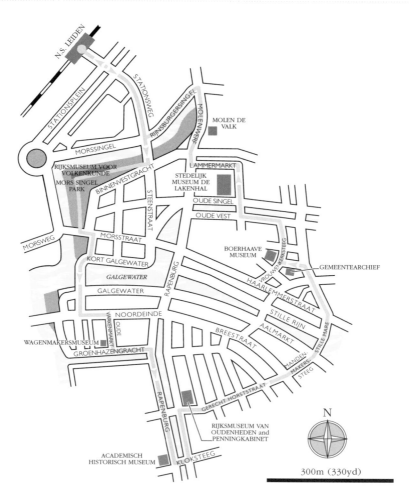

Folk and spokes

The National Museum of Ethnology is at no. 1 Steenstraat; the topics of its exhibits range from life in Mexico to hunting for food in the Arctic. A permanent exhibition highlights unsuspected differences and similarities between seemingly disparate cultures. There is a fine collection of dance costumes, masks and puppets from Bali.

Leave the museum by the west end of the park, at the corner of Eerste Binnenvestgracht and Morsstraat; facing away from the museum, turn left on Morsstraat, then immediately right. Cross the Galgewater and walk down the Weddesteeg to Noordeinde. Here, turn sharp left and take the second right down the Oude Varkensmarkt to the Wagenmakersmuseum (Cartwrights' Museum), at no. 13.

This former workshop was still making spoked wooden wheels for carts and barrows as recently as 1985; saws, chisels, planes and spokeshaves hang tidily by the old workbenches as reminders of virtually vanished skills, and there is a small collection of dog-carts, pony-traps and other antique wheeled vehicles.

Glorious alumni

Come out of the museum and turn right. Walk to the corner of Oude Varkenmarkt and Groenhazengracht and turn left, then go right at the end of the street onto Rapenburg. Walk along the canal, with the water on your left. Two blocks down is the Academisch Historisch Museum (Museum of University History).

The University of Leiden is the oldest in the Netherlands and is one of the most respected in Europe. It was endowed in 1574 by William the Silent to mark the relief of Leiden and reward the city for its heroic resistance to the besieging Spanish forces. William relieved the city by breaking the sea-dykes and sailing to the rescue on the resultant flood.

Among Leiden's professors and alumni are names like the philosopher René Descartes (1596–1650), the jurist Hugo Grotius (1583–1645) and the father of micro-scopy, Anton van Leeuwenhoek (1632–1723). Its small museum, with its collection of hats, gowns, faculty badges, anniversary souvenirs, photographs, prints and documents, shows how big a part the university has played in the life of the town for the past four centuries and more.

Antiquities and coins

From here, cross the Rapenburg to the Kloksteeg corner. Turn left and walk back up the opposite bank of the canal – with the water once again to your left – until you reach the corner of Houtstraat and the two museums housed in the complex at Rapenburg no. 28.

The Rijksmuseum van Oudenheden (Museum of Antiquities), founded by King William I in 1818, is the finest archaeological museum in the Netherlands, and has a superb collection of mainly Egyptian antiquities. It is built on the site of the former Hofje van Zessen. In the lobby looms the reconstructed sanctuary of Isis from the Temple of Taffeh; excavated in Egypt and dating from the first century AD, this was contributed to the museum by the Egyptian government in recognition of the Dutch part in the excavation and rescue of the ancient sites in Nubia, upper Egypt. There are superbly preserved Egyptian, Greek and Roman statues and friezes, mummies and inscriptions – among them one from Babylon, telling the story of the famous Hanging Gardens of Babylon, one of the Seven Wonders of the Ancient World. Perhaps more immediately interesting to visitors to the Netherlands is the section devoted to local archaeology, recently re-opened and displaying finds from pre-historic times up to the Middle Ages, including Bronze Age implements and Dark Age Frankish treasures. The 'Archaeology in the Netherlands' collection gives a complete overview of Dutch history, and most of the finds on show have been recovered by the museum's own archaeologists.

More bronze, gold and silver treasures are displayed in the Penningkabinet (Royal Coin Cabinet) collection, which shares the building with the Museum of Antiquities. Its hoard ranges from Greek and Roman coins to the gold dollars of the 18th-century Dutch East India Company, and includes also medals, antique banknotes and engraved gemstones.

Archives and anatomy

From here, turn into the Houtstraat and follow this thoroughfare round for several blocks as it curves to the left, changing its name successively to Gerecht Horststraat, Diefsteeg and Mandenmakerssteeg before it crosses the Rijn to become Stille Mare. Still bearing left, cross Haarlemmerstraat and Vrouwenkerkkoorstraat on your left before turning left into narrow Dolhuissteeg. Here, at no. 7, is one of the city's more obscure museums, the Gemeentearchief (City Archive). If aged documents hold no fascination for you – the archive has 4km (2½ miles) of shelves, with scrolls, parchments and charters stretching back to 1290 – at least glance at the prints and pictures on display before moving on. Among the archive's prouder possessions are letters bearing the signatures of Rembrandt and other famed citizens of Leiden.

At the far end of Dolhuissteeg, cross Vrouwenkerksteeg to reach the Boerhaave Museum, which is in a small side-street, at no. 10 Lange St Agnietenstraat.

The museum is housed in the former St Cecilia's Hospice and is named after Professor Hermann Boerhaave (1668–1738), the 18th-century botanist, chemist and surgeon. The collection is a hotch-potch of antiquated scientific and surgical instruments, including the earliest (18th-century) microscopes created by Anton van Leeuwenhoek and the earliest pendulum clocks built by the Dutch physicist Christiaan Huygens (1629–1693). Both were scientific revolutionaries. Leeuwenhoek's demonstration of minute particles and creatures too small for the human eye to see opened the way for new discoveries in medicine and biology. Huygens solved the mathematical and technical problems of the pendulum clock, presenting his first model to the States-General of the Netherlands in 1657 with his Treatise on Clocks and Pendulums. In 1675 he perfected the spiral regulatory spring, making it possible to build accurate clocks for the first time. His achievements extended far beyond horology, however: he discovered the rings and the fourth moon of the planet Saturn, and he can be regarded as the father of the wave theory of light – not to mention being the first person to discover polarization. Certainly he is one of the giants in the history of science.

Even more interesting, if a little spinechilling, is the reconstruction of an anatomical operating theatre. It is, literally, a theatre, with tiers of wooden seats to allow students a clear view of the dissection taking place on the operating table. A similar theatre is the setting for Rembrandt's *The Anatomy Lesson of Professor Tulp*, painted in 1632 in Amsterdam and now hung in the Mauritshuis in The Hague (see page 82). The anatomical theatre here is not for the faint-hearted – among its prized exhibits is a unique collection of skeletons.

Masterpieces and a windmill

From the Boerhaave Museum, turn left along Vrouwenkerksteeg, walk straight through Hazewindsteeg and, as you reach the canal, turn left onto the Oude Vest. Once known as the Bierkaay (Beer Quay), it was packed with small breweries. Breweries were always located along river- or canal-sides, usually on the outskirts of the city concerned, so that they had easy access to water transport for their raw materials and the finished product.

Cross the footbridge to Oude Singel on the opposite bank and turn left to the Stedelijk Museum de Lakenhal, housed in an imposing 17th-century building. This was originally, when built in 1640, the Cloth Hall, where the products of Leiden's thriving textile industry were first examined, to make sure they did not compromise the town's reputation, and then auctioned. It was also the headquarters of the town's Clothiers' Guild – the building's size indicates how powerful the cloth industry was. Murals show spinners, weavers and dyers at work.

The Lakenhal became the municipal museum in 1874. Make straight for the rooms at the back, where you'll find paintings by Rembrandt's teachers, Jacob Swanenburg and Pieter Lastman, his contemporary Jan Lievens and his pupil Gerrit Dou, as well as an early work by Rembrandt himself. There are also canvases by Jan Steen and by modern artists. *The Last Judgement* (1526) by Lucas van Leyden (1494–1533) is one of the gems of the collection. Other rooms display fine collections of pewter, silver, glassware and ceramics.

From the Lakenhal, turn left up the Molenwerf, which curves leftwards and crosses the Lammermarkt, taking you towards the unmissable tower and sails of the Molen de Valk (Falcon Windmill). A tall, circular brick tower, with a gallery just below sail-level, this grain mill was built in 1743. All seven floors are open, and there is a different display on each. The top three, which hold the milling machinery, offer fine views over Leiden. When the mill was functional, grain was hauled to the top floor and poured onto the grindstones below, emerging on the next floor beneath as flour ready for sacking. The last miller's living quarters, on the ground floor, have been preserved, with old furniture, paintings and photographs dating from the beginning of the 20th century.

From the mill, turn left along Rijnsburgersingel to Morssingel, then turn right over the canal bridge onto Stationsweg, thus returning to your starting point.

The Keukenhof

The Keukenhof is near the town of Lisse, 18km (12 miles) south of Amsterdam. You can make this walk only in the spring, but when the gloriously colourful Keukenhof gardens are in flower and open to the public it is a must.

Start/finish: Access by rail/bus via Lisse, with combined tickets available from Amsterdam Centraal Station

Length: 6km (4 miles) approximately; the garden covers some 28 hectares (70 acres)

Time: As long as you want!

Refreshments: Overcrowded and overpriced cafés in and around the gardens – perhaps best to bring your own

Open: End March–end May 08.00–18.30

Which day: Not weekends, if you can help it, because then the gardens are very crowded

Jacoba van Beieren (1401–1436), Countess of Bavaria and a daughter of the Hapsburg Imperial dynasty, laid out these gardens in the 15th century to provide fresh fruit and vegetables for her nearby castle. The site was acquired by a Dutch bulb-growing consortium in 1949, and its role as a tourist attraction is still secondary. Its main purpose is commercial bulb-growing; as soon as the plants have flowered they are chopped off short to encourage bulb propagation. (On the way to the Keukenhof you will have passed through the famous bulbfields of South Holland, seemingly stretching as far as the horizon, and have seen great heaps of discarded blossoms awaiting disposal at the side of the road.)

In their brief blaze of glory, however, the Keukenhof's six million tulips, narcissi, daffodils and hyacinths are a sight to behold. Great swathes of red, yellow, pink and blue blooms – the proud products of almost 100 leading Dutch bulb-growers – are laid out around the trees. Scattered here and there in the gardens are ten covered pavilions which, each year, display different newly created exhibits and arrangements.

For most visitors, the high-points are the two giant greenhouses that contain between them some 50,000 tulips, in a dazzling range of colour combinations. The Keukenhof's tulips are at their best from mid-April to mid-May, the daffodils from the end of March to late April, and the hyacinths from mid- to late April.

The Dutch obsession with tulips dates from the mid-16th century, when the first bulbs and flowers were brought back from their native Turkey (tulip means 'turban' in Turkish). They quickly became a national mania, and, when a Leiden horticulturalist named Johan van Hoogheland discovered how to hybridize them to produce different shapes and colours, tulipomania reached new heights. Multi-coloured varieties appeared on the scene: red, pink and white blooms were most highly prized. Bulb-growers set out to produce ever more flamboyant varieties, and prices soared. By the mid-1630s speculation in tulip futures was rife, leading eventually to a market crash which left many growers bankrupt before a more realistic attitude asserted itself.

Two centuries later, 'tulip fever' provided the French novelist Alexandre Dumas (1802–1870) with the background for his novel *La tulipe noire* (*The Black Tulip*; 1850). A black bloom still seems to be the tulip-grower's impossible dream − though the deep purple Black Parrot almost makes the grade, and eventually, no doubt, the ingenuity and ceaseless genetic tinkering of Dutch bulb-growers will create the real thing.

Enjoy the extravagant names of each variety; traditionally some of the finest blossoms are awarded a high rank − General or Admiral − as well as their grower's name. Others − like the Semper Augustus − are named in the imperial tradition, and others still after idols like Shakespeare, Queen Victoria or Florence Nightingale (a further Turkish connection).

Before leaving the gardens, you can buy a selection of bulbs to take home or have sent to you; bulbs sold for export are guaranteed perfect and virus-free.

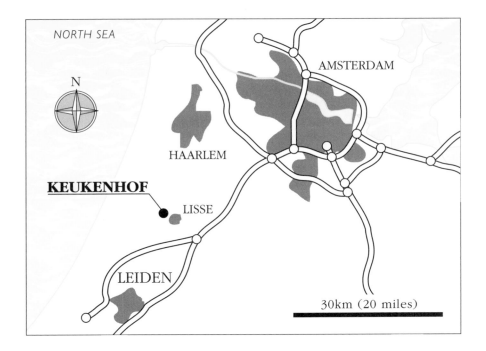

GLOSSARY OF COMMON SUFFIXES

Many street-name suffixes crop up again and again in every Dutch town, and a basic grasp of their meaning is a big help in finding your way around. Note that canal-names denote not only the canal itself but usually also the streets on either bank. Some other geographical suffixes are included in the list below.

binnen	*inner, inland*
brug	*bridge*
dijk	*ditch, canal, sea-wall*
dok	*dock*
dwarsstraat	*side-street*
eiland	*island*
gracht	*canal*
haven	*harbour*

kade	*canalside street or quay*
kerk	*church*
laan	*avenue*
markt	*market or market-square; often the main square of a medieval city*
plein	*square, often the central square of a city*
poort	*gate*
rak	*a reach or stretch of canal*
singel	*moat – originally a channel ringing the town and serving a multiple role as drainage ditch, sewer, transport canal and defensive moat*
sluis	*sluice-gate, footbridge across a canal sluice*
straat	*street*
wal	*sea-wall*
weg	*way*

PRACTICAL HINTS

Airports: Amsterdam Schiphol Airport: tel 020 601 0966; access by rail from Amsterdam Centraal and all Randstadt stations. NZH Travel operates a bus service every half-hour between the airport's arrival hall and the Hilton, Barbizon Centre, Marriott, Pultizer, Krasnapolsky, Holiday Inn Crowne Plaza, Renaissance and Barbizon Palace hotels.

Art galleries: Museums are listed at the beginning of each walk. There are also scores of private galleries, especially on the Spiegelgracht in Amsterdam and the Denneweg in The Hague; the local tourist offices have lists of the major ones.

Churches: Most are free and open 08.00–18.00.

Cinemas: Imported films are almost always in the original version with subtitles, rather than dubbed.

Eating out: Amsterdam has a huge choice of restaurants. The Netherlands is not noted for its indigenous cuisine, and lots of these establishments offer imported menus: Indian, Mexican, Chinese, Greek, Turkish and Indonesian restaurants abound, as do American-style burgers-beer-and-ribs joints. Head for the Jordaan district to get away from the repetitive formula and premium prices of the tourism-dominated centre.

Embassies and Consulates

Australia: Koninginnegracht 23, 2514 AB Den Haag; tel 070 3630938

Canada: Sophialaan 7, 2514 JP, Den Haag; tel 070 364 5800

United Kingdom: Lange Voorhout 10, 2514 ED Den Haag; tel 070 364 5800

USA: Lange Voorhout 102, 2514 EJ Den Haag; tel 070 362 4911

Health: EU nationals can get an E111 form (available in the UK from post offices) which in theory should cover you but in practice offers only basic care.

Payment must be made for medicines and some forms of treatment, then reclaimed on your return, which process takes ages. In any case, private health insurance should be part of your holiday insurance cover. Ambulances, doctors, dentists and pharmacists can in emergency be contacted on 5555555.

Loos: There are very few public loos. There are good, clean facilities at museums and in restaurants. Cafés – on every street corner – provide a third alternative, and stations a fourth.

Markets: Amsterdam has more than a dozen street markets, all of them offering various snacks and selling everything from livestock to antiques. Opening days differ. Those featured here include the Antiekmarkt de Looier (see page 58); Looiersgracht Rommelmarkt (see page 58); Spui Art Market (see page 50); Waterlooplein Market (see page 32); Bloemenmarkt (see page 50); Noodermarkt Boerenmarkt (see page 42) and Albert Cuypstraat Markt (see page 46). A full list of markets and opening times is available from the city VVV.

Museums: The major museums in Amsterdam and its satellites are listed, with their opening times, at the head of each walk. In general, most major museums are closed on Monday; smaller museums may have different opening hours, which can be obtained from the local VVV. Here are the addresses and telephone numbers of the major Amsterdam museums:

Museum Amstelkring: Oudezijds Voorburgwal 40; tel 6266604

Amsterdams Historisch Museum: Kalverstraat 92; tel 523 1822

Allard Pierson Archaeological Museum: Oude Turfmarkt 127, tel 5252556

Anne Frank Huis: Prinsengracht 263; tel 5567100

Bijbels Museum: Herengracht 366; tel 6247949

Filmmuseum: Vondelpark 3; tel 5891400

Geels & Co Koffie en Theemuseum: Warmoesstraat 67; tel 6240683

Joods Historisch Museum: Jonas Daniel Meijerplein 2-4; tel 6269945

Kattenkabinet: Herengracht 497; tel 6265378

Madame Tussaud Scenerama: Dam 20; tel 6229949

Nationaal Vakbondsmuseum: Henri Polaklaan 9; tel 6241166

Netherlands Maritime Museum: Kattenburgerplein 1; tel 5232222

NINT Technology Museum: Tolstraat 129; tel 5708111

Het Rembrandthuis: Jodenbreestraat 4-6; tel 6384668

Rijksmuseum: Stadhouderskade 42; tel 6732121

Rijksmuseum Vincent van Gogh: Paulus Potterstraat 7; tel 5705200

Stedelijk Museum: Paulus Potterstraat 13; tel 5732911

Theatermuseum: Herengracht 168; tel 6235104

Tropenmuseum: Linnaeusstraat 2; tel 5688215

Verzetsmuseum: Lekstraat 63; tel 6449797

Werf 't Kromhout: Hoogte Kadijk 147; tel 6276777

Museum Willet-Holthuysen: Herengracht 605; tel 523 1870

Parks: Amsterdam is notably short of inner-city green space. Three main parks – the Vondelpark (see page 60), the Plantage (see page 65) and the Sarphatipark (see page 46) – are described in three separate walks.

Public Transport: Public transport in Amsterdam and the Randstadt is excellent; route maps and information on system-passes and tickets are available from central stations and VVV municipal tourist offices.

Trams offer the widest network and the least complicated way of getting around town. Underground Metro trains in Rotterdam and Amsterdam are quick and efficient, but the network is limited. Buses are the slowest way of getting about and the network is more complex and less easy to use.

Railway stations: Amsterdam Centraal (tel 620 2266) is the rail terminus for Schiphol Airport, the Randstadt towns, and international rail services. For further information on stations and rail services contact Netherlands Railways, Marketing International, PO Box 2025, 3500 Utrecht, tel 030 354652, fax 030 319621.

Taxis: These are relatively expensive and, in view of the excellent public transport on offer, are not always worth taking; they are not always much faster than trams or trains.

Telephones: Buy a phonecard at a post office, newsstand or hotel. Some street phones also accept credit cards.

Tourist Offices: City tourist offices (VVVs) usually have their information office at or very near the main station; they offer a wide range of information leaflets, maps, hotel and restaurant listings and accommodation booking services. There is a small charge for some of these.

In the Netherlands

VVV Amsterdam, PO Box 3901, 1001 AS Amsterdam, tel 020 5512512

VVV Den Haag (The Hague), PO Box 85456, 2508 CD Den Haag, tel 070 3618888

VVV Zuid Holland (Delft and Gouda), Markt 85, tel 015 131942

VVV Leiden, Stationsplein 210, 2312 AR Leiden, tel 071 146846

VVV Rotterdam, Coolsingel 67, 3012 AC Rotterdam, tel 010 4023200

VVV Utrecht, PO Box 19107, 3501 DC Utrecht; tel 030 331544

Overseas offices of the Netherlands Board of Tourism

Australia: NBT, 6th Floor, 5 Elizabeth Street, Sydney NSW 2000, tel 02 247 6921

Canada: NBT, 25 Adelaide Street East, Suite 710, Toronto, Ontario M5C 1Y2

United Kingdom: Netherlands Board of Tourism, 25-28 Buckingham Gate, London SW1E 6LD, tel 071 630 0451

USA: NBT, 355 Lexington Avenue, New York NY 10017, tel 212 370 7367

What's on: Time Out Amsterdam, published monthly, offers a comprehensive listing of every imaginable event and activity in the city.

Where to stay: The Netherlands Tourist Board abroad and local tourist boards in the Netherlands provide lists of accommodation at all levels, from the cheapest youth hostel, campsite and dormitory accommodation to luxury hotels. Booking well ahead is very strongly advised, especially if you plan to travel in spring or early summer, or at weekends. In high season accommodation is hard to find at short notice.

BIBLIOGRAPHY

Some books worth reading before or during your trip:

The Penguin Guide to Amsterdam, ed. Vincent Westzaan (Penguin, 1990), written by a group of Dutch journalists and authors, gives a highly personalized view of the city.

Holland, by Adam Hopkins (Faber and Faber, 1988), is an impressionistic portrait of the country, its history and people.

The Embarrassment of Riches, by Simon Schama (Collins, 1987), is a scholarly but accessible interpretation of Dutch culture during the 15th- and 16th-century Golden Age.

The Diary of Anne Frank (various publishers, on sale at the Anne Frank House) is Anne's moving account of her life in hiding from the Nazis and a powerful symbol of the Holocaust.

INDEX